ANASTACIA TOMSON grew up in Johannesburg and gradu-
ated as a medical doctor from the University of Pretoria. She
has worked as a general practitioner in both the public and
private sectors, and as a freelance journalist. Anastacia has
a passion for activism and advocacy, with a specific interest
in promoting access to health care for transgender and gender
non-conforming individuals. For more on Anastacia's activism,
please visit www.doctomson.co.za/blog, www.facebook.com/doc.
ana.tomson and http://twitter.com/anaphylaxus.

ALWAYS ANASTACIA

A TRANSGENDER LIFE
IN SOUTH AFRICA

ANASTACIA TOMSON

Jonathan Ball Publishers
Johannesburg & Cape Town

Published in South Africa in 2016 by
JONATHAN BALL PUBLISHERS
A division of Media24 Limited
PO Box 33977
Jeppestown
2043

ISBN 978-1-86842-713-0
ebook ISBN 978-1-86842-714-7

Every effort has been made to trace the copyright holders and to obtain their permission for the use of copyright material. The publishers apologise for any errors
or omissions and would be grateful to be notified of any corrections that should be
incorporated in future editions of this book.

Twitter: www.twitter.com/JonathanBallPub
Facebook: www.facebook.com/JonathanBallPublishers
Blog: http://jonathanball.bookslive.co.za/

Cover by publicide
Photography by Tanya Rudman de Sousa of TRPhoto (www.trphoto.co.za)
Design and typesetting by MR Design
Printed and bound by Creda Communications
Set in Century Schoolbook and Trade Gothic

*The names of all of the people who appear in this book have been changed to protect
their identities. The point of writing about these experiences is not to name and
shame any particular individual, or to call individuals out for their behaviour,
even if they acted in ways that were grossly insensitive or prejudiced. Some of the
encounters that I describe involved specific people, but they could just as easily
have happened with anyone else. They were a product of systemic misunderstand-
ing and intolerance, which I hope to address with this book.*

AHHM, I love you. I know that you know.

To Gabriella and Amilia, with all of my love.

To the tiger who always has my back.

To those in whose footsteps I follow,
And to those who follow in mine.

To the child who had to grow up too fast.
You always did the best you could.

And the day came
when the risk it took
to remain tight in a bud
became more painful than
the risk it took to blossom
– *Elizabeth Appell*

Contents

Preface

Being out

When I first understood that I needed to transition in order to live, I started thinking about the kind of life that I would pursue. Specifically, I spent much time thinking about the prospect of 'going stealth'.

It was a real temptation, the idea of packing my bags and disappearing to some other town with no ties to the life I had pretended to live. Leaving behind my old name, my traumatic childhood, my confusing adolescence, and those first hollow years of my adult life.

I could settle somewhere new, where no one would recognise me.

Transition is a gruelling process. There is hardship at every turn: dealing with ignorant and insensitive health-care professionals to gain access to treatment, trying to convince government departments to amend identity documents, fighting against a conservative society that would sooner write people off as freaks than try to understand their struggles or ease their strenuous journeys.

Many people act as if they have rights to transgender people's bodies, asking us intimate and inappropriate questions and expecting answers. Some touch without permission, and become offended when we rebuke them. People fixate and quiz us on our sexuality. They ask after our genitalia, whether we've had surgical procedures, whether we intend to. How we knew, whom we've told, whether we sit or stand to pee, how we have sex. Transgender people who wish just to sink into anonymity and live the peaceful life for which they have fought have my unending empathy and respect.

There was a time when I wanted that too – when I used to say that I was not an activist. That I did not need to make my voice heard to make a difference. I was content to initiate change through my work, and felt that my activism was quiet and non-confrontational.

But, as I grew more confident in my identity, I discovered that not only did I have a voice, but that it insisted on making itself heard. I was a proud woman and a proud feminist. Discrimination and oppression based on gender, gender identity, sexual orientation, or race had always worried me, but I had never known how to address them. I had never felt that I had the agency to speak out, or anything worth saying.

As my self-respect grew, I re-examined my priorities. I wanted to live the life that I felt I deserved, in peace. But I also wanted people to understand the lengths to which I had gone to be seen for who I was. I was not ashamed of being trans, and I did not want to have to live in fear of my 'secret' being discovered someday.

I knew there would be a price – that to make some kind of difference to those who faced struggles similar to mine, I'd have to lay bare the intimate details of my life. But I knew, also, that doing so would bring me freedom. My dark 'secret' could hold no power over me if it wasn't a secret at all.

So, I made my decision. I came out – first individually, to friends and family, and then to the world. I made no attempts to hide who or what I was. It was not easy, but embracing my truth has allowed me to strengthen so many of my bonds and relationships. Of course, a few have suffered. Some friends, even ones who are mentioned in this book, have grown distant from me. Some of them still associate with me, though our dynamic has shifted irrevocably; others refuse to talk to me at all. But my connection with those who have stood by me is stronger than ever.

I chose to combat prejudice and hatred with empathy and understanding. I am many things: a woman, a friend, a doctor, a confidant. I am transgender. Sometimes I am afraid and overwhelmed. I am a human being, and these are my experiences. I hope you enjoy sharing them – my pain and my happiness.

I entrust my secrets to you. All I ask for in return is your compassion.

With pride

Day 0, 1 July 2015

I rub the sleep from my eyes as I open them, squinting at the bedside clock. Eight o'clock — earlier than I expected it to be. The first weekday morning in a long time that I haven't been roused by an alarm clock. The sensation is novel.

I feel the morning chill of the Johannesburg winter against my face, as the scent of freshly brewed coffee wafts from the kitchen into my bedroom. I am grateful that I neglected to turn off the timer switch, despite my plans to sleep in. I gaze briefly at the bare, off-white walls of my bedroom, reminding myself that I still haven't got around to hanging the prints of the wildlife photographs I used to take while working in Mpumalanga four years ago.

As I crawl out of bed, it takes a few moments for the reality to settle in: today is the first day that I am free of the expectations of maleness to which I have been subject for so many years. For months, I had been presenting exclusively as female in every setting barring my workplace. My job has been the last outpost of that old shell of a life.

I pull back the curtains and stare, for a moment, out my bedroom window, watching the palm trees in my neighbour's yard swaying in the breeze. The feeling is surreal: that I no longer have to act every day, switching back and forth between voices, mannerisms, vocabulary. That I am free to live the life I believed would never be mine to live. It is overwhelming. I feel relief, but even so, I know that I can't comprehend just how enormous this change has been.

Yesterday was my last evening at the practice. It was heart-wrenching and bittersweet. I left without fanfare, without the opportunity to say my goodbyes properly. That chapter of my life ended anticlimactically, with a whimper far more than a bang. I still feel that I need closure, but that will have to wait for another time. Right now, I am just relieved to be absolved of that job and its responsibilities.

I stand in front of the mirror as I remind myself that I no longer have to wear the 'uniform'. I can grow my nails, and paint them. I am free, finally, to have my ears pierced. I can use the voice that I've spent so many hours meticulously cultivating with Michelle, my speech therapist. I no longer have to hide my disgust at being called *boet* or sir, or tolerate any references to my deadname.

I have fought hard, held back for decades by a body that did not fit and an identity that did not belong. At first, it had seemed like transition was a vague and unattainable aspiration, a romantic ideal that was incompatible with reality. But now – after five months of hormone therapy, countless sessions of painful laser hair removal and multiple appointments with doctors and psychologists – it is very much a reality.

This is far from the end of the road, however. Hormone therapy will be lifelong. At some stage, I envision perhaps undergoing surgery, or surgeries. I continue to wait for the Department of Home Affairs to make the changes to my name official and to amend my legal gender. But none of these details seem to matter terribly much in the face of my new-found freedom. Transition is no fanciful daydream – it is the life that I am living, and no longer has to share its time with falsehood.

Overnight, 'he' has ceased to exist – the performance ended, the character retired, the uncertainty, fear and pervasive disquiet replaced with confident calm. I have never been without my positive attributes: I was always smart and compassionate, kind and caring, honest and just. But I've had to temper many of those qualities with my forcibly guarded, defensive nature. Now, they can blossom unhindered. All of my favourable traits are still present, but accompanied now by so many more.

For the first time, I am allowed to be myself, with no reservations or restrictions. And I am proud.

* * *

A week ago, I was sitting at my desk when the phone rang. As usual, I panicked briefly – a throwback to my days of working shifts in a busy rural hospital in the mountains of Mpumalanga. In those days, a phone call was never good news; someone had died, or was in the process of dying, or needed to be rushed to theatre. Since moving to an upmarket private practice in the northern suburbs of Johannesburg, phone calls are usually nothing more serious than a pharmacist checking the details of a prescription. I took a moment to remind myself that this phone call would be nothing worth worrying about.

Except, it was. When I answered, the voice on the other end asked me if I knew that there were photos of me on the Internet dressed as a woman. I wanted to answer, 'That's because I *am* a woman,' but for the next few moments I was paralysed with fear.

For six weeks prior to that phone call, I had not left the house in men's attire except to go to work. I had scoured away every reference to my deadname on social media. Even at work, I had begun to make concessions to make sitting behind my desk more bearable. I had taken to wearing my nails longer, and I'd started to grow my hair. It didn't surprise me that someone had recognised who I was – what did surprise me was that it hadn't taken longer.

I panicked, overcome with fear that my dreadful 'secret' had been revealed. As a child I, too, had been subconsciously conditioned to think that there was something abnormal about transgender people. The idea that transness is deviance, that being trans is intrinsically wrong, has become less pervasive in media and contemporary culture in recent years, but many of us still harbour such sentiments.

My panic and humiliation stemmed not from truth, but from internalised notions imprinted on me as a child growing up in a world where anyone who wasn't cisgender and heterosexual was considered an aberration. But I was no aberration. I was better than I had ever been – warm-hearted, compassionate and liberated, and unafraid to care, speak, love and be loved.

My terror subsided. I knew that word was spreading, and I could imagine what people would say about me. The words flashed through my mind. Cross-dresser. Transvestite. Tranny. He-she. Shemale. Sex change. A slew of inaccurate, derogatory, or obsolete terms. I needed to set the record straight as a matter of urgency.

I cleared my head with a few deep breaths, and willed my frenzied pulse to slow. Then, I began to type.

We live in a society in which people thrive on the shame of others, clamouring after gossip and scandal. Maybe it makes us feel better about ourselves – reminds us that we're not the only ones with dirty laundry.

My journey began a long time ago. It's been filled with challenges that many people will never have to face. That's not to say that my challenges are more significant than anyone else's, but simply that many people will never be able to relate to them.

I have no choice in the matter of who I am. I made no decision to be this way; it's intrinsic and immutable. The only choice I made was whether to live honestly or to die pretending.

I am not ashamed. People like me face preconceptions and prejudices. We're stigmatised, ostracised and ridiculed for who we are. We are victims of assault and abuse. Many of us lose our lives to violence or suicide.

4

I am a good human being. I am compassionate, empathic and caring. I stand up for the people about whom I care and the principles in which I believe. I work hard. I'm a good friend, sister, daughter and doctor. I refuse to sell myself short any longer.

Some of you out there will try to scandalise what and who I am, and will want to make a spectacle of me as you would an animal in a zoo. Say what you wish. Come and gawk at me. Everyone who is close to me – friends, family, even my employer – has known this truth for months. Everyone who matters in my life knows me, accepts me, loves me and supports me.

Right now, I am fulfilling the final commitments of the person I once pretended to be. Once that is done, my double life will be over. This is who I am, and who I have always been. I neither offer nor owe any apologies or explanations. The days of shame and pretence and insecurity are behind me. If you are looking to satisfy your craving for scandal and guilt, you will not find it here.

This post is public, as are many others of mine. Whether you are a friend, an acquaintance, a patient or a stranger, I leave this here for you to see. Pass it around, share it, send it to everyone you know. The truth may persecute some, but it liberates me.

I did not choose to be who I am. But today, and every day, I choose to live.

With pride.

Within minutes of posting, I began receiving phone calls and messages from patients. The outpouring of support took me by

5

surprise: messages that praised me for staying true to myself, and that commended my courage for being open about what I was experiencing. Patients and old school friends slowly began to get in touch with me as the days passed.

I had always been accustomed to avoiding attention, and now found myself at the centre of it. To know that for every person who talked *to* me there were tens that were talking *about* me was unsettling. But I was secure in who I was, and the details of what people were saying about me lost their significance. All traces of fear had left me: this liberation was exhilarating.

Now, standing in front of my mirror, naked and exposed, I don't feel vulnerable. It doesn't matter what anyone thinks of me. I am worthy. Majestic. Freedom is mine at last.

* * *

The first day of the rest of my life is upon me. The gravity of this has yet to sink in. For the few mornings that follow, I wake and drag myself out of bed, often before I remember, gleefully, that the life I'd pretended to lead is a relic of the past.

The future belongs to Anastacia.

Potpourri

Day –252, 22 October 2014

I heard about the support group from a friend I'd met at a dinner party. Originally I had thought that *she* was a cisgender lesbian. I later learned that *they* (a chosen gender-neutral pronoun) were in fact genderfluid, and non-binary, and self-identified as 'hella queer'. *Their* hair had been cropped short, and what little remained had been dyed a vibrant colour – if memory serves, at that time it was blue. Sam dressed in clothes that I'd normally regard as androgynous, but in comparison to their partner's attire, they looked quite femme. They were a student at the time, on the verge of qualifying as a homeopath. Their partner was an accountant, dressed in chinos, suspenders, a collared shirt and a necktie, with cropped hair and a smile that was ever-so-slightly mischievous, but still quite reserved.

It was a group dinner, an informal mixer organised by an Internet community. I found the two to be refreshingly intelligent, with wonderful senses of humour and a world view that didn't clash with mine. I'd always felt uncomfortable at social gatherings, but I quickly warmed up to the pair of them.

I continued chatting with Sam online in the days following the dinner, and they suggested to me that I should attend a meeting of the support group. I was still coming to terms with my identity at the time. Like many, I had grown up with the misconception that gender and sex were one and the same – a fallacy that masquerades as an immutable truth.

The group's meetings had been advertised as a safe space, a gathering of non-judgemental people whose identities spanned the length and width and depth of the gender spectrum. They met on Wednesday evenings, the venue rotating between the homes of the various members.

On this particular evening, the meeting was hosted by one of the group's founders. She lived with her parents in a lavish house on an equestrian estate; I was told that the estate had the highest density of horses in the world, though no reference for the claim was cited.

The house was astonishingly large, sprawling out from the entrance hall in every direction. The word 'mansion' did not seem out of place. The decor had an African bush theme – each room was littered with wooden sculptures of warthogs or antelopes or rhinos and the door handles were fashioned to look like elephant tusks. I had not yet met Michaela's parents, but I suspected they had more money than taste.

I was neither the first nor the last to arrive. A few of the group members were already seated on the couches in the lounge, cups of coffee in hand and side plates with biscuits or pastries in front of them. Michaela waited outside to greet me, dressed casually in azure skinny jeans, a pair of white-toed sneakers and a T-shirt with a skull print on it. Her turquoise hair cascaded down the sides of her face, which broke into a wide smile. I'd met her the week before, when I had been her plus one at a social engagement. We hugged in greeting and she led me inside, to a seat next to the one she'd reserved for herself.

The meeting began; each attendee gave an introduction. We sat in a circle, the introductions proceeding in a clockwise direction. I was sure it wasn't accidental that I would be last – Michaela must've sensed my apprehension, being in such an unfamiliar environment, and was trying to put me at ease.

Bryan was first. He introduced himself as a trans man, preferring the pronouns 'he' and 'him'. He was short, but stocky and muscular; his arms were adorned with tribal tattoos, and his jaw covered in blonde stubble. If I had to guess how long he'd been on hormones, I'd have said for his whole life. Testosterone works quickly, and it clearly agreed with him.

Taylor – who, at that point, still went by Luke – identified as genderqueer, and preferred gender-neutral pronouns. Today, they wore a cream dress with black heels, their hair short, in a boyish style.

Becca was a photographer and a model. She had striking features and an imposing physical presence, a throwback to her days as captain of the high-school rugby team. She joked freely about the life she used to have, and the surprise it had caused her classmates when they learnt who she really was.

Next to introduce himself was Steve. He was one of the older attendees, and did not identify as trans. He was, in fact, the father of a trans girl who was not in attendance that evening – she was still recovering from a surgical procedure. Steve was unassuming and pleasant enough, the first to admit that he didn't always understand all of the issues that were discussed in the group, but was putting a great deal of effort into trying to.

I had met Margaret before. She was a friend of Sam's and the other co-founder of the group. She wanted top surgery so she'd have breasts over which she could wear a binder, and bottom surgery so that she could 'pack' (wear a prosthetic phallus, used predominantly by trans men). 'Fucking with society's notions of gender' further was one of her greatest aspirations in life.

Dianne exuded an air of grace and patience. She was softly spoken and chose her words carefully, clearly taking the feelings of others into consideration before she spoke. She seemed to enjoy a great degree of respect from the other members, who always spoke of her fondly.

Then it was my turn. Hearing all the introductions brought home to me the fact that although these people all shared a common thread, each one had an identity and experiences that were unique. Society often wants us to fit into neat little compartments, but the group of glorious misfits in whose company I sat were a testament to the obsolescence of that concept. I still had no idea what to say about myself, but was, by now, at least convinced that there was no right or wrong answer.

I have always maintained that not everything or everyone needs to have a label. There is no conceivable way in which a singular term can accurately encompass all the facets of a group of individuals; by labelling them, we leave ourselves susceptible to preconception and prejudice. If your label was, for example, 'transgender woman', people would often assume that you'd gone through a phase trying to be a gay man, that you'd insisted on wearing dresses in your youth, and that you'd tried to mutilate your body with various bladed instruments at some point in your life to escape from the intense psychological torment that you suffered by virtue of having a penis. While for many those experiences may be true and valid, they are far from universal.

At the same time, though, I realised that labels were not without their benefits. They encouraged us to search for and embrace commonality, and they gave us a frame of reference, albeit sometimes a vague one, for some of our experiences. And, probably above all else, they made it easier to find support. After all, it's much easier to find meaningful results on Google for a term like 'genderqueer' than it is for 'gender that changes sometimes and doesn't quite fit in with being either fully male or female'. The label can be empowering, as long as its limitations are acknowledged.

I had not yet found my label.

'My name is Staci,' I stammered, painfully aware that at that moment, in my mind, I looked very little like a Staci, 'and I'm … gender … something. I don't know yet.'

'Don't worry,' said Taylor, 'it will all fall into place with time.'

'Nice to meet you,' Bryan offered. 'I hope you feel welcome here.'

Michaela silently reached an arm across my shoulders and squeezed gently.

The subject of that night's meeting was hormone replacement therapy. I participated, to an extent, by virtue of my medical knowledge rather than my personal experiences. Some of the members were on hormones, and had been for a while. Others were not, and had no desire to be. Some were eagerly awaiting a time when they would be able to start. Again, I was reminded that no two people's experiences are ever identical.

That I was dressed as a man that night, in beige trousers and golf shirt, didn't matter. I was who I was, whatever I may have been wearing – nothing could change that. I knew the space was a safe one, but I was still apprehensive. Although the clothes had felt wrong for some time, there was a degree of comfort in the familiarity of playing such a well-rehearsed role. At one point, Steve glanced at me from across the circle and smiled. One of the ladies had just made a remark about struggling to get her eyeliner right. Steve was also looking for commonality; in a circle of trans people, I suspected he was feeling quite isolated. It took conscious effort, but I managed to give him a sympathetic nod. It drove home the extent to which my appearance betrayed me – I'd spent my whole life being read as male, and it was becoming increasingly apparent that I'd always been anything but.

The meeting came to an end, and we all began to say our goodbyes. I exchanged hugs with each of the members, feeling at ease by now. Steve offered me a handshake, the universal male greeting. I reluctantly reached for his hand, compromising my own discomfort to avoid offending him. I felt like I was betraying my own nature, and I was. It had taken me 29 years to realise that I didn't have to.

It may have been my first meeting with the group, but I decided, as I left, that it was the last one at which I would arrive cross-dressed.

Missed a spot

Day –245, 29 October 2014

It had been more than five months since the first time I'd gone for a wax. Prior to that, it had always been a razor, or a tube of foul-smelling hair-removal cream. The nicks and cuts were frustrating, and the occasional chemical burns, though mild, were horribly uncomfortable. I gradually learnt which areas of my skin were the most sensitive and adapted my technique accordingly.

I remember always being embarrassed by my body hair, even though I may not have known why. I had shaved my chest once before, when I was still a student, for anatomy class. We had been divided up into small groups of seven or eight for a simple exercise: one volunteer from each group would disrobe from the waist up and have his chest covered in cling wrap so the other students could use markers to draw the outlines of the thoracic and abdominal organs.

I knew I would have to be the volunteer for my group, as I was the only student in the group who was not read as female. The night before the activity, I had frantically shaved my chest in the shower, trying desperately to remove all traces of hair. I'd never been comfortable exposing myself in front of people to whom I wasn't very close, and I had been mortified by the thought of doing so with a hairy chest. By the time I was done, my skin was red and raw. The hairs were mostly gone, but prickly stubble remained. To my relief, no comments were passed the next day. I remembered it being horribly itchy as it regrew.

By now, I'd kept my body hairless for longer than I could remember. The rashes and the bumps and the burns were all less uncomfortable than the notion of letting my hair regrow. That hair was proof of somatic betrayal – a ubiquitous reminder of testosterone, that ill-fitting molecule that coursed through my veins.

I had never been especially hairy, and for that I was glad. But the struggle against the relentless regrowth was a constant one. I remembered having to allow the hairs to grow before my first wax – if they weren't at least a centimetre long, the wax would have nothing to grip onto, and the hair would not be removed. That was the longest I'd allowed them to be in months, and watching them grow was demoralising.

Being smooth always left me with a sense of well-being, irrespective of how that smoothness was achieved. Over the months, the waxing had become less painful, and I'd figured out the perfect cocktail of painkillers and meditation techniques to make even the most sensitive areas bearable. I'd had two or three different therapists as time went by, some of them better and some worse.

For the past few weeks, I'd been seeing Melissa, a young blonde girl with a demeanour that was friendly though not effervescent. Her friend and colleague Kirsty had been treating my chest with laser. Kirsty was a fair bit shorter than Melissa, and quite a bit bubblier. The two were always glad to see me when I arrived at the spa, and they made sure that I knew I was one of their preferred customers.

Today, I had come in just for a wax. Melissa was gentle, and good at what she did, and a decent conversationalist. I lay naked on the treatment bed, covered with a towel. The room was spacious and comfortable, with wooden fittings and a pale tiled floor. Ambient lighting in the ceiling slowly shifted through a spectrum of colours, while new-age spa music competed with the hum of the air conditioner. A faint scent of vanilla floated in the air. The spa was just off a bustling main road, but the noise of the street was the farthest thing from my mind; I drifted away from the taxis and the newspaper vendors and the wire-animal sculptures.

Melissa entered the room and, after exchanging greetings and how-are-yous, she set about her business beginning, as she always did, with my right leg. She'd start with the foot and the calf and work her way up until she'd completed the whole leg, before moving on to the other side. She occupied herself by making small talk, though she caught me off guard when she began on my left foot.

'I like the colour you had on your toenails.'

I thought I'd managed to get it all off after my shower that morning. *Must've missed a spot*, I thought.

'Oh do you? I'm glad, it's one of my favourites,' I replied, without missing a beat.

'I prefer purples myself,' she said, 'but yes, I think it's pretty.'

There was no judgement or animosity on her part, and no nervousness or guilt on mine. It reminded me how comfortable I'd become with the idea of who I was.

It wasn't until my next session that she worked up the nerve to ask about who or what I was, though it took her until my left thigh to do so.

'So, you're gay, right?' she asked.

'Well. Maybe. But I'm not a gay man. I'm transgender,' I replied.

'Oh ... I used to date a man who cross-dressed,' she ventured.

'Um, that's a different thing,' I said. 'I'm not a transvestite. I don't dress up for kicks. I'm transgender – it means that actually, I *am* a woman.'

She nodded in appreciation.

She asked me about the process of transitioning, and the effect that hormones would eventually have. By the time I was done explaining, she'd just about finished my right arm.

'Well, I think it's cool that you're going to be yourself.'

I didn't think it was especially cool. I was just doing what I needed to do to survive. Colourful hair dye is cool – transitioning is a challenge, and a commitment, and often an intense source of anguish. I knew she meant well, however, and I took the comment in the spirit in which it was given.

'Thanks, so do I,' I replied, as she moved on to my left arm as if nothing out of the ordinary had happened.

14

Not man enough

Day −325, 10 August 2014

I woke up before Jennifer, as I often did on Sunday mornings. The worst of winter was behind us. I would have to go to work in a few short hours; every second Sunday, I'd see patients between 10:30 and 12:30. My back had been worrying me – the muscles seemed always to be in spasm. Jennifer had arranged an appointment for us at a nearby spa in the afternoon, for a back and shoulder massage that I desperately needed.

* * *

She had been distant recently. Always consumed with her writing, always stressed out from the job she'd recently started, always glued to the computer screen or her mobile and never willing to talk. Earlier in the year, we'd been to couples therapy – not because we were in any kind of crisis, but because we'd been starting to talk, after all this time, about marriage and settling down. We needed to determine how we'd reconcile our religious and cultural differences, especially if we were to have children.

She'd expected me to be apprehensive about going with her to therapy; I had been anything but. I went with her week after week and bared my heart, even when it was difficult. I made an effort to present an honest picture of myself and of my interactions with her. I felt that we'd grown in our ability to compromise and communicate and understand, even though our personalities were often at odds. In the few months that followed, we'd done so well, speaking openly and often and not easily becoming angry or frustrated about trivial things.

It had taken a lot of effort for each of us to try to understand the other.

It is human nature to interpret other people's behaviour in the context of our own. Jennifer was whimsical, and extroverted, and she spoke before she thought. Her mind changed like the weather, and if she were making a decision about something, she'd vocalise every thought. It often gave me the impression that she'd flit about, unable to stick to a decision; I'd have to remind myself that she was still thinking her way through it.

In contrast, I had always been more methodical, systematic, calculated. Faced with a decision, I'd carefully and quietly consider it, speaking my mind only once I'd arrived at a conclusion. I was still guarded with my emotions then, even with her, though to a far lesser extent than with anyone else. It was easy for her to construe my behaviour as being aloof, or as an unwillingness to engage. It confused her that I'd speak only when I'd made a decision.

I'd learnt to understand that sometimes Jennifer just needed a sounding board – that if she said something rash, it was more likely to be what she was feeling in the moment than her conclusive feelings. I'd been much more patient with her, reminding myself not to react but to give her the space she needed to run through everything in her mind.

I'd hoped she'd also come to the understanding that I was trying to let her in, that it was difficult for me to be as open and expressive as I would like to be, and that even if there were times when I wouldn't say anything, it didn't mean that I wasn't feeling anything.

But despite all of our progress, the past few weeks had been difficult. We lived in the same house, but at times it felt as if she were more my roommate than my partner. I knew she was under a lot of stress, and I was desperately trying to connect with her, to be there for her. I'd sit next to her while she typed away at the computer, looking at her pleadingly while she ignored me.

She'd told me a few weeks before that she wanted to move out and live on her own. That she needed her own space. That she wanted us to stay together, but thought our relationship would be healthier if we lived apart for a while. She'd assured me that it would be temporary, and did not mean that she no longer wanted me. Forever still meant forever.

One characteristic of my father that had defined many of his relationships was a lack of trust. Every one of those relationships had been toxic and abusive. I had made a decision to trust Jennifer – to trust that she would be faithful, to trust her when she said she wanted us with all of her heart.

A short time before the discussion about her moving out, she'd wanted to discuss the idea of an open relationship. I'd said to her that if she was going to be sleeping with other people, I'd need to know beforehand. Everything would have to be on the table. I knew she had never been monogamous in the way I was, and I wanted her to be happy. But I could not abide deception or dishonesty. I had no desire to sleep with other people, but if she did, I wanted to do my best to be okay with it.

She had cheated on me once before that I'd known about, not long after we had first become a couple. She had confessed immediately, and I had been devastated. It had happened only days into our relationship, but it had torn me apart, and I had been ready to write the whole thing off as another failed romantic endeavour. She had begged for forgiveness.

My heart had always been soft, which is why I'd learnt to guard it so well, using walls of cynicism, sarcasm and pessimism to protect my fragile feelings. She had known the way in, even then, disabling my defences. Like an expert burglar, she had done it without my even having realised. And so I had forgiven her, and we had carried on. I had promised her that if she ever cheated again, I would leave: no debate, no negotiation.

* * *

That Sunday morning, I poured myself a cup of coffee as I always did, and sat down with it in front of the computer that we shared. We had separate accounts, and we'd each log out when we were done with our business so the other could log in.

She had been the last to use the computer on the preceding evening, and had forgotten to log out. As I sat down and switched on the monitor, I saw an open chat box. I thought nothing of it, and started moving the mouse to close it. I stopped abruptly when I caught a glimpse of its contents.

17

Your hard cock. Wet cunt. Fuck you so hard. In your pussy.
It went on.

The phrases shot out at me from the screen. I hadn't yet read the messages in full, but already my heart was racing. I tried to rationalise and justify – she could not have been sexting behind my back. Surely it wasn't possible.

But I could no longer ignore it. She was, and had been for some time. I scrolled up to the naked pictures and videos of each other masturbating that they'd shared. I felt numb, then hurt, then livid. In a fit, I went through the rest of her chats, her e-mails and her files. It was a guy she'd met through one of her writer friends, who'd started flirting with her a few months back. She'd told me that she'd cut ties with him, that she wasn't interested. I had trusted her.

She had made plans to video chat with him again that morning, shortly after I'd left for work. She was still pretending to be asleep when I left.

My patients knew that something was wrong. I must've been asked four or five times that day if I was sick, or if something had upset me. She sent me messages to say good morning and to remind me about the massages she'd booked as if nothing had happened.

I returned from work and said barely a word to her; we left soon afterwards for the spa. She tried to make conversation. In her mind, nothing had changed. We were together, as we had been for a while. She was cheating, as she had been for a while. And I didn't know, as I hadn't for a while.

The massage brought me no relief. My discomfort with my own body had always made it difficult for me to relax beneath the hands of a stranger. This encounter, of course, was worse than usual. I was as polite as I could manage to be to the staff at the spa, but I did not relax in the slightest. I left with more of a spasm than that with which I'd arrived.

By now, the tension was palpable. Jennifer must've known that something was wrong. And because she didn't ask me, I knew she must've known what it was. I waited for her to say something to me, for an admission that never came. After her betrayal, I felt she owed me a confession at the very least. But it became clear that she was going to make me confront her. That I would have to ask her all the questions, one by one, until I was exhausted or satisfied.

My every question carved fresh wounds into me as I asked it. Who she'd been with, what she'd done, when it had started. I desperately wanted to understand, and couldn't. She denied it at the time, but later I learnt that she had cheated before, two years earlier, by sleeping with a mutual friend.

I resented that she had cheated, but more than that, I resented that she made me ask her. That she made me piece together the details, bit by painstaking bit. That she watched me, suffering and tormented, with no mercy. There was no admission, no apology, just lies, cruel and uncaring. She started to cry; I turned away.

I had put so much into our relationship from the day it had started until its end. I had stood by her through changes of jobs and problems with her family. I had driven her to hospital when she'd overdosed on prescription painkillers. I'd tried not to blame her, to be supportive and understanding and compassionate.

Before the break-up, I'd already had some inkling of the process going on within me. But in its traumatic aftermath, stripped of the protection of gender and roles and societal expectations that the relationship had once afforded me, my thoughts had begun to solidify. I could no longer hide from who I was.

In time, it became easier for me to understand. I had hoped to be everything that Jennifer wanted. I could, perhaps, have been – except that she wanted a man, something I had never been, even when I'd looked the part. On some level, she must have known it. Before any of the ideas had been articulated properly, the feelings and emotions had started speaking for themselves.

She had wanted our relationship to end, but she hadn't had the courage to kill it herself. Whether I was a man or not, she knew I would never break a promise to her. She cheated, I kept my word; it ended there and then.

Had I waited another week, it would have been seven and a half years to the day.

Ownership

Day –237, 6 November 2014

I lifted my shirt and looked in the mirror, a silly grin plastered onto my face. I still couldn't even walk past the mirror without stopping to take another look. Over the past 12 days, I must've caught myself staring hundreds of times. I'd slip my hand under my shirt at work, reminding myself of the small step I'd taken in claiming ownership of my body.

As far as body modifications go, a navel piercing may not be the most exciting. But for someone who'd customarily been straight-laced, it felt like a big step – one that was thrilling and reckless and empowering.

I'd come out of a seven-and-a-half-year relationship scarcely two months earlier. I was hurt, and angry and frustrated. I'd been looking for something I could do, something completely out of character. I wanted to divorce myself from the straight-and-narrow that had always felt so comfortable to me.

I had thought about anonymous casual sex. The activity itself didn't hold much appeal for me, but I desperately wanted to feel desired. I dispensed with that notion when I realised that I didn't have the faintest idea where to meet someone for a casual encounter and that, even if I did, I didn't want to be intimate with anyone with whom I didn't have an emotional connection. I was craving intimacy, not physicality.

Drugs and alcohol were out of the question. I had always been quite fond of my mind, and the idea of altering it with substances had never excited me in the least. I'd never had a hangover in my life, and this wasn't the time to start. I wanted something that would empower me, not leave me regretful.

I had briefly considered the idea of a tattoo but, ever the prag-matist, I'd wondered how it would look in decades' time when the canvas had lost its youthful firmness. At that moment I could think of no statement or image that I'd want emblazoned on my body forever. It was the sort of decision that needed time and consideration, if ever I was going to make it.

I'd been toying for a while with the idea of a piercing. It seemed like the ideal indulgence. Something just outlandish enough to give me the rush I was craving, but with a very low likelihood of long-term regret. I'd have loved to have done my ears, but that was impractical – I needed something more discreet.

Recently, I'd grown a little fonder of my midsection than I had ever been before. I'd noticed that I was a lot more trim in the mirror than I had been in my mind. I'd been overweight as a child, and though my body had long since shed the excess kilo-grams, my mind still carried them around. My waist was on the small side – long before starting hormones, my figure and pro-portions tended more towards the feminine than the masculine.

It was the ideal place for a piercing – it wouldn't be visible unless I wanted it to be, just a hidden reminder that I was starting to take ownership of my body and my life. I'd be able to show it off when I wanted to, but it was always, first and foremost, going to be for me.

The piercing was still fresh, and it was swollen and a little tender. The piercer had been shaking and sweating as he'd driven the needle through my virgin flesh. He'd fumbled the ball bearings as he tried to screw them on to the edges of the bar. The place itself had been hot and dusty and far away, though my friends had recommended it without reservation. I told myself that he'd been shaking because he'd only recently started working there, but I knew with very little doubt that he'd been under the influence of some or other substance.

I realised even then that the piercing was off-centre, at an angle, and generally far too shallow. Objectively, he'd done a terrible job. I clung to the hope that it may start to look a little better as it healed, though I suspected I'd eventually need to remove it, let it heal and have it redone. But for now, it hid under my clothes – a secret affirmation of my identity, a mark on my body that designated it as belonging to me, when for such a long time I'd felt like it hadn't.

I looked at the talisman that hung from my navel for a few moments more, then dropped my shirt and walked away, my silly grin replaced by a wide smile.

Independent woman

Day −2 707, 2 February 2008

Rain poured down. My feet had started to ache, each step through the mud consuming more and more willpower. Originally, I'd thought, obstinate as ever, that I may just walk the length of the highway until I reached Pretoria. Maybe a part of me thought that my father or stepmother would come to their senses and come after me to take me back home.

I finally reached the highway, taking shelter under a bridge from the relentless rain. Slung over my shoulder was a duffel bag with a few clothes to see me through the next few days, and not much else. I slumped into a heap beneath the bridge, and dialled Leo's number.

*   *   *

I had avoided confrontation with my father for 23 years. I'd walked on eggshells to keep him happy, neglected my relationship with my mom and my brother, and sacrificed any semblance of a social life I may otherwise have had at school or university. I had lived with him since the age of nine, but had dealt with the fear and anxiety all my life.

Many of my early childhood memories had been lost, but I did remember him screaming and shouting at my mother, slamming doors and storming off. I didn't know when things had become tense between the two of them. They still seemed happy together in some photographs, but my earliest memories were of conflict between my parents.

Both my mother and my father had been married before, and each had had a son in those marriages. My half-brothers were 10 and 11 years older than me. My father had always had a problem with Leo, the son who wasn't his. He used to call him 'the rat'. It's no surprise that I'd always got along so much better with Leo than with the other one.

After the divorce, I had initially lived with my mother. My father had soon manipulated me and bullied her into having me stay with him instead. Once he had me living under his roof, he had seized the opportunity to try to turn me against my mother and her side of the family, speaking ill of them at every opportunity. I had not been as easily swayed as he would have liked, however. Even at a young age, I'd been one to think for myself.

My father had many prejudices. He was a racist and a bigot, and was shameless about it. He had tried to inoculate me with his intolerance when I had been too young to know any better. When you are young and innocent, your father is a hero in your eyes. As a small child, I'd repeat at school the diatribe I'd hear him spout at home. When I was old enough to understand what he'd been teaching me, I was disgusted with myself, and with him.

When it became apparent that belittling my mother in front of me was insufficient to achieve his aims, he became passive aggressive. Any mention that I made of my mother or Leo would result in him muttering obscenities under his breath. As punishment, he'd ignore me, pass hurtful remarks, or just stomp around the house in an obviously bad mood. If I wanted to see or spend time with my mom or my brother, I would have to muster the courage to tell him and endure his wrath after the fact. Often, I'd simply refuse to see them at all, just to avoid the inevitable fallout.

My father was threatened by independence; he preferred his women battered. I never knew him to be physically abusive, towards me or anyone else, but he was manipulative and controlling and horribly insecure. He needed to see himself as a knight in shining armour, a role much easier to play as the partner of a woman whose self-esteem and independence had been dismantled.

He was a man of average height, rotund, with a grey-black beard that looked immaculate after a trip to the barber, but quickly became unkempt. His hair was long, despite his having been bald on top for many years. His complexion was reddish, and he was frequently out of breath. He always wore a gold chain around his neck and a ring on his little finger, and carried a gold ballpoint pen in his shirt pocket. His skin was oily and hairy, his fingers short and chubby.

He was an attorney by profession. He had been my mother's lawyer when she had separated from her previous emotionally abusive husband. My stepmother (who was thirty or so years his junior) had also been in a physically abusive relationship. She had started out as one of my father's employees.

My father never could tolerate a strong, independent woman. He would not stand for my mother socialising with her friends. He would demand to know where she was at all times, and would chastise her for 'gallivanting' if she went out alone. After their separation, he'd intimidated her with lawyer's letters written in legalese unintelligible to the average person to ensure that the divorce proceedings worked out in his favour.

My stepmother had always been meek, a mousy woman with a pasty complexion. Her face was littered with red blotches, when she didn't cover them up with foundation. She wore her hair short, in a style you'd expect of a much older woman. She usually dressed in high-waisted designer jeans that cut her figure in just the wrong places. She had all kinds of physical tics, manifestations of her constant anxiety. She had clearly been badly scarred by her previous marriage. When she'd become ready to move in with him, my father had bought a house in a gated suburb in Benoni. The town had never been renowned for its affluence, but this was certainly one of its fancier neighbourhoods. The residents had been almost exclusively white. They drove big German cars, and their houses all had perfectly manicured lawns, separated from the realities of everyday South Africa in the early 2000s. The house was sprawling – far bigger than I could understand any house ever needing to be. Worse, it was a good thirty kilometres away from my school in Glenhazel, one of Johannesburg's foremost Jewish bastions. I didn't remember the justifications he gave at the time for buying there – likely some concocted tale of rising property values in the area. In reality, the house's location kept me at a sufficient distance from the rest of my family. As an added benefit, it meant that I lived far enough away from my school friends to make social interaction outside of school itself impractical.

His strategy was as it had always been – he isolated and demeaned to foster the dependence that fed his twisted, fragile ego. He did not plan to give up his paltry semblance of control easily: when the time came for me to start university, he decided that I should study in Pretoria, some fifty kilometres away, and insisted that I continue to live at home. I was to phone and check in whenever I left and whenever I arrived.

* * *

The camel's back had broken: 23 years of silent suffering, of enduring and persevering and carrying on, shattered in the space of moments. My father was terminally ill, and had lain in his bed in the room next door to mine. My stepmother and I had gone to great lengths to show him as much support and care as he would allow. In the preceding few months, I had forced myself to start saying 'I love you' to him, to hug him, and to find time to talk with him, despite my busy life as a medical student.

Just two days earlier, he had been admitted to hospital. He had flown into a rage close to midnight, demanding to be brought home immediately. My stepmother and I had gone to fetch him. I'd been exhausted and frustrated and trying to study when I'd heard him complaining from the adjacent room. He'd accused me of slamming doors and running taps in the middle of the night, deliberately trying to disturb him and cause him suffering.

I was often up late studying, but I took great care to be as silent as possible. I knew there was no substance to his vindictive tirade. I had taken every care to try to ensure his comfort, and I was being castigated for it. Not to my face, but from the room next door, though loudly enough to be for my benefit.

I had known then that the floodgates were about to open, and that my life was about to change forever. I had burst into his room, demanding that he make his hurtful allegations to my face if he had the backbone to do so. I'd admonished him for his cowardice, telling him that the people who loved him were doing their utmost to show him care and love and tenderness, and that he was pushing them away.

26

He'd threatened me with bodily harm, told me several times to drop dead, and demanded that I get out of his house. All the while, my stepmother had stood in the doorway, giggling nervously as I had stood up to him – not just for my sake, but also for hers.

I'd packed a bag, run to the car and driven off into the night, seeking refuge in a parking lot somewhere. I pushed the driver's seat back and cried myself to a restless few hours of sleep.

In the morning, a message from my stepmother had flashed onto the screen of my mobile phone. It was a cold and impersonal demand to return the car, which had been given to me for my eighteenth birthday, or it would be reported to the police as stolen. I had driven back to his home, angry and tearful, and left the car with its keys in his garage. As I'd begun walking, it had started to rain.

* * *

From the shelter of the bridge, I told Leo briefly that I was no longer welcome in my father's house. He did not seem surprised to hear it. He asked where I was; a few minutes later, I was in his car, on the way to his home. He told me not to worry, that everything would be okay, and that he would always have my back.

I did not see my father again until his funeral, less than two years later. I made an effort to reconcile with him a few months before his death, but he remained bitter and obstinate until the end. I attended his funeral and said Kaddish for him for a month after his death. I am sure it was more than anyone else did.

* * *

In later years, I would learn that my conception had not been entirely planned. My father had desperately wanted a child, ostensibly as a means to control my mother. She, at 39, had thought herself unlikely to be able to conceive, and had indulged him by having her contraceptive device removed. A few months later, she was pregnant with me, and he had the weapon he had so desired.

Later still, my mother confided in me that my father had hoped to have a little girl, something she reminded me about some time after I had come out to her. She thought it ironic that his wish may actually be fulfilled, so many years after his death.

I knew that he would not have been pleased. After all, my father never could tolerate a strong, independent woman.

Dysphoria

Day –221, 22 November 2014

I gazed at my naked reflection, scrutinising the body before me for what felt like hours. It was pale, almost bleached. Its face was gaunt, and its shoulders sloped and drooped, despondent. The chest, broad but flat, gave way to arms that were muscular and unattractive. A narrow waist and, lower still, a thin, silver barbell on the navel. Wider hips, but a silhouette that ran straight up and down nonetheless. Flabby thighs, and shrivelled flesh limp between them, forgotten.

And all over, small, dark hairs visible beneath fair skin amid scattered red bumps where the hairs had begun to grow in instead of out.

With each moment, my heart sank a little further.

The body was mine, though I seldom liked to believe it.

* * *

Dysphoria is a formidable adversary. It's a concept I have always struggled to explain to those who have never had the misfortune of experiencing it. It is a shapeshifter – it moves and changes and adapts. It is sometimes a vague, nagging sense of unease, and at other times an open wound. It is debilitating, opportunistic and merciless.

There was a time when I told myself that I had never experienced dysphoria. In truth, I had experienced it for as long as I can remember. It used to manifest as a non-specific feeling of discomfort – a sensation that eyes were always on me, judging me, measuring me against some unseen metric of acceptability, and finding me lacking. I'd been self-conscious about my body for a long time, though I originally imagined that this emanated from a general lack of self-esteem.

I had known for some time that I felt more comfortable seeing myself dressed as a woman. I loved the softer fabrics, the wider selection of colours, and the flattering cuts; the flowing dresses, the detailed tops, the pencil skirts and the jumpsuits. Everything just seemed to fit better. I didn't always see a beautiful woman looking back at me, however; all I could see were the masculine features I tried so desperately to hide. As I stood naked in my bedroom, picking out all of the characteristics that make me unhappy, I recognised the dysphoria for what it had always been.

To me, dysphoria has been the monster under my bed: a vague, malevolent presence lurking in the darkness. I have, sometimes, almost been able to ignore it, but at the back of my mind I have known that *something* lay hidden, an overbearing feeling that I just didn't fit in, though I did not know why. I used to tell myself that I was simply 'not like other guys', that I was different, but still normal – that nothing was wrong.

Recognising that what I was experiencing was, in fact, dysphoria was like shining a torch under the bed. Claws and fangs and scales lay revealed, and could no longer be ignored. Vague discomfort was replaced by anxiety and distress, which were all too specific.

Some days were better than others. There were times when I'd admire my tapered waist, my delicate wrists, or my long, milky legs. I'd feel hopeful and optimistic and beautiful. On other days, I'd know from the moment that I dragged myself out of bed that the mirror would be my enemy. I would struggle to find any trace of that comforting femininity, and would be repulsed by my own incongruent maleness.

The oscillations were unpredictable. They just happened, out of nowhere, leaving in their wake spells of depression and hopelessness that could last for weeks. Although my friends were wonderfully supportive, they could bring me no consolation. No amount of complimenting or reassurance could provide relief.

As time passed, I developed techniques to help myself cope. I'd pick out the physical features that I liked, and make a point of admiring them. I'd spend hours in front of the camera taking self-portraits, keeping only the ones that flattered me and made me feel good about my body. I kept my skin hairless and my toenails painted; I grew my fingernails out ever so slightly; I adorned my navel with jewellery – nothing too obvious, but small concessions that were sources of strength and affirmation in times of anguish.

Dysphoria, however, is adaptive and resilient. It may disappear for a while, but it returns with greater intensity. The attractive becomes harder to see, and the unsightly more difficult to ignore. Dysphoria is a symptom of an incongruence between body and mind. The symptom can sometimes be controlled, but it cannot be cured without addressing the cause.

I needed to take steps to reconcile my body and mind. Attempting to change the mind is fruitless and frustrating, but hormone therapy had, up to now, been a faint and far-off aspiration, a desire that I'd often written off as being impractical.

*   *   *

Exposed in the middle of my bedroom, face to face not just with my troubling reflection but with my fears and frustrations and hopes, I had nothing left to gain by pretending. I knew in that moment that I could not continue to live in a body that had always betrayed me and would continue to do so.

It had been four weeks since I had acknowledged that I had 'gender issues', a term whose lack of specificity was somehow comforting. At first, I admitted to myself that I did not identify wholly as male – that I recognised in myself a distinct feminine energy, and that the recognition had always been there. That it was stronger than I had imagined.

I'd held out for as long as I could, clinging to the idea that there was still some maleness in me that I'd be able to accept. I was scared of what it might mean if I couldn't.

As my reflection looked back at me, I knew that no doubt remained. The body did not fit. My entire life did not fit. Transition was not a choice – it was a necessity. Somewhere in the weeks that had passed – between the break-up and the support group meetings and all of my reading and research – the notion that any maleness existed somewhere deep inside me had slipped away. That safety net, that familiarity, was gone.

Instead of grief or doubt, I felt only serenity.

Reminiscence

Day –219, 24 November 2014
I held in my hands an old photo, taken when I was in primary school. In a sea of smiling young faces, I managed to pick out my own, sullen and frowning. As I thought back, I struggled to recall a time when my body had not made me feel self-conscious and ashamed.

* * *

I was a slight child with no great physical prowess. I did not like to touch, and I especially did not like to be touched by others. They labelled me 'tactile defensive'. Of course, I was too young to understand what the term meant.

In my early school days, I had always done my utmost to find reasons not to participate in sports or physical activity. When I was unsuccessful, I'd find myself in the changing room going to great lengths to hide myself and exposing as little flesh as possible. These were primary school days – I should have been too young to feel ashamed of my body. I never had the confidence that the other children had about their bodies. Mine did not belong to me, and I was resentful that I belonged to it.

When puberty came, it brought changes that amplified my discomfort. Ugly, wiry hairs started to grow, thin but unmistakable. The smooth skin of my face slowly gave way to scattered patches of fluff, then stubble.

I had little contact with girls. The religious Jewish school I attended split the genders long before puberty to avoid impropriety. The girls' classrooms were situated all the way on the other end of the campus, and the breaktimes of the two schools were strategically structured so as not to overlap. If I'd had more contact with the girls, perhaps I would have started to realise why the changes I was experiencing were so uncomfortable.

The boys around me were like a foreign species with an alien language. Their culture, customs and rituals were bizarre and made little sense to me. They bullied each other, delighting in the shame, humiliation and physical pain that they could wreak upon one another. They were obsessed with sex, as teenage boys are, and their jokes were off-colour.

Underneath all the stereotypical behaviours, the nuances of maleness were lost on me. Perhaps I was too young to understand it properly, but so much of it seemed to come so naturally to my peers. It unsettled me – I wasn't used to things that I didn't understand. I had no mutual understanding with my classmates, though I recognised on some occasions that it was better to pretend than to admit this. Nonetheless, I don't recall having meaningful friendships with any of the boys.

I was much more comfortable keeping to myself. I spent breaktimes indoors reading or getting a head start on my homework while the others engaged in whichever rowdy pursuits took their fancy. I knew I was an outsider. Keeping my distance did enough to mitigate my discomfort. I was smart and excelled academically. More than that, I was willing to help my classmates with homework or tutoring. My academic prowess was a commodity, and I traded it for exemption from the boyish pursuits in which my classmates may have expected me to engage.

At one point, I tried to compensate for my shortcomings with rigorous weightlifting, thinking – on some level – that the antagonism between my body and me may lessen if my body conformed better to the physical 'ideals' of maleness. The gym itself was an uncomfortable place, the changing rooms in particular; I avoided them when I could, and felt horribly awkward when I could not. My resentment, shame and irrepressible desire to hide were manifestations of my dysphoria, which I had not known at the time.

In my adulthood, I continued to shy away, trying to make my body as invisible as I could. Friends would invite me over to their swimming pools and I'd sit covered up in the shade, refusing to disrobe no matter how sweltering the heat. I took to wearing long, baggy trousers. Shorts I avoided completely; outside of my own shower, I was never bare chested.

It was not only my body that troubled me. It was the way people treated me, and the things they expected of me. The words and titles by which they called me that always felt so discordant. The commonality I was supposed to share with other men that had always been absent. The peculiarities of intercourse that seemed so simple to others, but which were so complex to me. The clothes that didn't fit and that never felt comfortable. My role models, who had largely been women. My closest friends, who had been girls.

So many insignificant details, taken on their own – each one easily ignored, but together, a body of indisputable evidence.

I spent a great deal of time and energy discounting the possibility that I could be anything but cisgender. I tried to convince myself that I may be quirky or unconventional, but that was the extent of it. For many years, I refused to think about sex and gender, not admitting for a moment that they may be two different concepts, rather than two words for a single concept.

My dysphoria went unacknowledged as it grew ever more intense and began to manifest as self-loathing. Objectively, I knew that I had many positive attributes, but always felt inadequate, that I deserved calamity in place of success. I never envisioned myself as one day being satisfied with my lot in life. I felt like I had some great intrinsic failing for which I needed to atone through self-sacrifice.

Friends and family I kept at a distance, unwilling or unable to burden them with my emotions. For years, I refused to give myself permission to cry, all the while telling myself that this was my due. I was content to know where I didn't fit in and to endure life as a perennial outsider. I didn't even begin to consider that there was a place in which I could feel comfortable.

The way in which I came to start questioning the fundamental concepts that I'd always taken for granted was gradual and, in some ways, serendipitous. It was a culmination of coincidental factors – stumbling across news articles, happening upon blogs, meeting people who also did not conform to the standards I'd once thought were rigid.

I started to think of myself as freed from these unspoken rules and requirements, which felt far more pleasant than I could ever have imagined.

Diagnosis

Day –208, 5 December 2014

The psychiatrist's waiting room was somewhat less lavish than I had anticipated. A few simple chairs stood at the end of a corridor, divided into two banks by a small table on which a filter-coffee machine and a handful of mugs rested. Behind the reception desk were what seemed like an inordinately large number of filing cabinets, and a few shelves cluttered with books for sale – mostly about fashionable high-fat, low-carbohydrate diets.

The coffee looked as though it had been in the machine for long enough to render it unfit for human consumption. Fortunately, I needed to wait only a few minutes before The Psychiatrist was ready to see me. Despite years of medical education designed, supposedly, to turn me into a well-rounded doctor free of the fetters of prejudice and stigma, I was intimidated by the prospect of submitting myself to any sort of medical examination, least of all a psychiatric one.

Dr Kevin Ross was younger than I expected him to be, and better dressed. His face was plump, its roundness further accentuated by his saucer-shaped spectacles. He'd been recommended as trustworthy, sympathetic and knowledgeable about gender issues. His praises had been extolled by those who had worked under him as well as those whom he had treated. I'd also been told that the spectacles served a cosmetic purpose only, somewhere between a fashion accessory and a prop.

As he led me into his office and extended his hand in greeting, I reminded myself that the reason for my visit was not uncommon, at least not for him. Yet when he asked me why I'd come, the words still stuck for a second in my throat.

'I have gender dysphoria.'

I don't know if I'd ever said it out loud before that moment – certainly not to a stranger. It took a few seconds, but relief swept over me. I had put the concept into words; I'd voiced it, out loud, and the world had not ended.

My interrogation lasted the better part of an hour. The questions ranged from the most mundane to those that were, in retrospect, wholly inappropriate. I gave the most comprehensive description that I could of my childhood, my parents, my romantic relationships, my sexual proclivities, my hobbies and my career plans. I think he may have even asked what I'd eaten for breakfast that morning.

He seemed disappointed by my lack of suicide attempts, substance abuse and prior psychiatric illness. No self-harm, no borderline traits, no mania. He was especially perturbed that as a child I hadn't played with my sister's Barbie dolls or worn her dresses. It didn't seem to matter to him that I did not, in fact, have a sister.

I think what I'd feared most about this consultation, and many of my future consultations with my fellow doctors, was the idea of having to prove my identity. In the medical profession, it's all too easy to become caught up in the pursuit of scientific evidence to the detriment of a patient's humanity. It's much easier to treat a laboratory result than an individual, after all. Of course, there was no blood test or scan that could diagnose me. Gender dysphoria is 'confirmed' by details in the patient's experiences and life story. For those who've never experienced it themselves, it becomes an exercise in pattern recognition – picking out bits and pieces of a narrative that fit in with a preconceived notion of the 'typical' experience of a transgender person.

Maybe my narrative was less typical than it could have been – but it was mine, and it was valid, and I was not going to alter or embellish it for anyone. It had never been easy for me to drop my guard. But I'd made a decision to stop hiding, and I clung to my resolve in the face of the unending barrage of intimate and often embarrassing questions.

So, in the forty-five-odd minutes for which he'd known me, this man had become privy to more personal information than I'd ever shared in my life. His demeanour hovered somewhere in between sympathetic and impassive throughout – to his credit, I only caught him daydreaming a handful of times. My life story, scrawled illegibly over three or four pages, sat in front of him as he removed his fake glasses and stared off into the distance for a few moments.

'I can see that you're insightful, and thoughtful, and that you've given this a lot of consideration. You'll need to start seeing a psychologist,' he said, as he began rummaging through his drawer for a pile of business cards. He started to rattle off a series of names, all therapists whom he trusted and admired for a variety of reasons. He struggled to finish a sentence about any one of them before interrupting himself to extol the virtues of another. Tangentiality, circumstantiality, derailment ... I had to remind myself that I was not there to diagnose him.

By the time I was ready to leave, I knew, at least, what my next step would be. He'd decided which therapist he deemed best suited to see me: the doyenne of gender, a veritable expert in her field. He'd also offered to prescribe antidepressants on at least three separate occasions, not hesitating to tell me that in an ideal world, they'd be pumped into the water supply.

I left his office relieved, knowing that the first step towards medical help was now behind me.

In luck

Day –154, 28 January 2015

The building was cold and austere, a dark, drab grey on the outside and a lighter but equally drab grey within. The corridors were narrow and stark. Nothing but the medical suites and laboratory depots that the building housed would survive in these cramped, clinical spaces.

A signboard just inside the entrance told me that Dr Barker's office was on the first floor. I climbed the spiral staircase and followed the corridor to the gate that marked the entrance to his rooms.

I had been in therapy for about two months and for the past few sessions already, my psychologist Meryl had been wondering what to do with me. Therapy had brought no revelations or breakthroughs – I'd already given much thought to my gender identity, childhood trauma and interpersonal relationships. I had always been introspective and contemplative. I had not been decompensating and I was not in crisis, which was, perhaps, unusual for patients in my position.

I had never been accustomed to letting people in – I had a bad habit of self-sufficiency that was a product of the combination of childhood isolation and latent dysphoria. It had taken a great deal of effort just to make it to support group meetings, and to start to share with people, but doing so had also proven liberating. Not only that, but it gave me the opportunity to start making some new friends and to allow myself the freedom to relate to people even outside the setting of the group.

My dysphoria had been worsening unceasingly since I'd acknowledged that I was, in fact, trans, and I was increasingly anxious to address it. After hearing Meryl remark during session after session about how well adjusted I was, and how much clarity I had about my situation, I had asked her if she'd feel comfortable contacting the psychiatrist again with a view to referring me for hormone therapy. She'd been happy to oblige, and Dr Ross had contacted me shortly thereafter. He was looking for an endocrinologist who'd be willing to help, and assured me I'd hear from him soon.

Another two weeks had passed, and my frustration was mounting. The dysphoria was relentless, and it started to impact my mood and my social life and my attempts at self-care. Meryl had agreed that I was ready, and saw no merit in waiting. It was at her suggestion that I took matters into my own hands, contacting Dr Barker and scheduling the appointment.

He was a general practitioner, but he was spoken of very highly by many of the transgender friends I'd met in the support group meetings. He was said to be sympathetic and understanding, and competent in prescribing hormone therapy. I sent him an e-mail to introduce myself. He replied to say he'd be amenable to treating me, and I scheduled my appointment soon thereafter.

I was anxious in the days leading up to the appointment, not knowing what to expect. I trusted the recommendations and knew that there was no conceivable reason to think that he would not be approachable and compassionate. But I was apprehensive, nonetheless; I surprised myself by getting a full and restful night's sleep before my appointment.

When I phoned to make the appointment, I'd been informed about the consultation fee for a first visit and told to have the sum in cash – a credit card transaction would incur a surcharge. When I entered the waiting room, I noted that the whole operation looked far less clandestine than the payment instructions had led me to believe. I approached the reception desk, introduced myself and began filling out the paperwork.

The waiting room was less pretentious than I expected of a practice in the heart of Sandton. It was stark and cramped. I took a seat between the tables that were strewn with old magazines, trying to avoid eye contact with the other waiting patient. Within a few minutes, a tall blonde man came to call her through.

Eventually, she emerged from the consulting room, and Dr Jeff Barker beckoned me to follow him, greeting me warmly. Somehow, I had imagined he would be older. He wore his beard short, and his hair was neatly combed. He was lean, though I thought I could detect the slightest hint of a paunch beneath his shirt.

I took a seat, and he asked about the reason for my visit. I explained that I'd e-mailed him the previous week about transitioning. It took him a few moments, but uncertainty was followed quickly by recollection.

'Oh yes, I do get a lot of e-mails, but I think I know which one you're talking about!' he said.

I had felt my heart thumping in my chest since I'd entered the building; my unease had not yet subsided.

'Yes,' my voice quivered. 'I was referred to you by Meryl.'

I braced myself for an interrogation, expecting to be asked the typical panel of questions on which medical professionals typically fixated: At which age did you know? Did you play with girls' toys? Did you long to wear dresses as a child? Are you sexually attracted to men? When last did you hack away at your genitals with a saw to escape your emotional distress?

Barker surprised me – he smiled, said 'Okay' and thrust forward a business card for a surgeon in Thailand as he launched into an explanation of how the surgical options for gender confirmation procedures in South Africa were exceedingly poor. He began explaining in earnest how the aim of hormone therapy is to increase levels of circulating oestrogen while diminishing those of testosterone. He mentioned the basic recipe that he liked to use, and told me we'd start at low doses and gradually work our way up.

He remembered at some point that he'd have to examine me, and I climbed onto the examination bed, removing my shirt.

42

He measured my blood pressure, listened to my heart and my breathing, and squeezed behind my nipples to determine whether I had any breast tissue that may respond favourably to hormone intervention. Scarcely two minutes later, I was clothed and seated in front of his desk again.

He explained that I was fortunate to have good skin, aside from the acne scarring, and that I was in luck, because he also happened to carry out cosmetic laser procedures in his practice. He promised me he'd be able to minimise the scarring and would give me a good rate. He mentioned that my brow was not overly prominent and my jaw wasn't too big – he seemed convinced I'd make an acceptable woman someday. If my nose worried me, he said, it wouldn't be a problem – he just happened to know a brilliant ENT who was great with rhinoplasties and voice surgeries. And I was in luck, because his rooms were just downstairs, in the very same building.

My hairline, he said, should respond favourably to hormone treatment. He was very excited to see the results as time went by, but if my hair refused to regrow, I needn't worry – he knew a wonderful hair transplant surgeon. And I was in luck: he may even be able to arrange a discount for me.

My superb luck had not yet run out. When the time came for dealing with Home Affairs ('Usually after about a year of hormone treatment,' he said), he had a contact in the Department who'd be able to expedite the process of changing my name on my legal documents. I didn't enquire about the cost of this fast-tracking service, but by then I was confident I would be lucky enough to get a reduced rate.

He recommended a sperm bank for preserving genetic material, and told me which shampoo he used to prevent hair loss. He made vague mention of some other transgender patients with whom he thought I may get along quite well, with less regard for their privacy than one may have hoped. He ticked off the necessary blood tests on a form, and wrote up the prescription for the initial medication.

I thanked him for his help, took all the forms and business cards he'd given me, and stood up to leave. He reminded me about the laser skin therapies he performed as he held the door open for me, and I assured him I'd be in touch. I hoped he was as good a doctor as he was a salesman.

I settled my account with his receptionists and made for the nearest pharmacy, enduring rush-hour traffic to get there. The pharmacist was a little puzzled about why a fairly typical-looking man was filling a script for oestrogen, progesterone and testosterone blockers, but before I had a chance to answer his question he'd come to the conclusion that the medication must be for my wife.

I saw no need to tell him that I did not have one.

When I returned home, I unpacked the medicines and set them on the kitchen counter. I longed to start swallowing them then and there, but knew I needed to visit the sperm bank and do Dr Barker's baseline blood tests first.

I sat in front of my computer and browsed the Cryobank's website. Just as I reached the page that contained their contact information, a notification flashed onto my screen – I had an e-mail waiting. It was from Dr Ross.

I spoke to Dr Williams, an endocrinologist, today, and she is willing to see you. Please just Google her rooms' telephone number. She'll know to expect your call.

Having waited so long already, delaying another week or two for the endocrinologist would be survivable, I thought. I packed the medicine boxes into one of my cupboards, looking at them wistfully as I closed the door.

Handshakes

Day −963, 10 November 2012

I'd spent the morning running around from shop to shop, trying to get the requisite supplies. Jennifer and I enjoyed having guests over, but it was something we did infrequently, so we were usually underprepared. Charcoal, meat, salad, ice, more meat, dessert, drinks. It had always been in my nature to over-cater. I'd often blame it on my being Jewish, but whatever the reason, I always felt more comfortable knowing there would be too much than worrying that there may be too little.

Many of our friends were couples themselves. Often, I'd remark to Jennifer before any guests arrived that I knew I would have to put on an act to fit in with the company we expected. I had not yet made the leap to understand that this stemmed from gender dysphoria, but I was consciously aware that I needed to 'perform'. I found even the anticipation of it exhausting. The low-pitched rumble of routine conversation interspersed with laughter, the weight of the braai tongs in my hand, the occasional sound of a can being opened, the mingled scents of seared meat and smoke threatened to overwhelm my senses; I had to focus on the performance, and not let myself be distracted by the props or the setting,

I kept a box of latex gloves in the kitchen for unsavoury tasks, like scrubbing the grill. I was still that tactile-defensive child, which was a fancy way of saying that I didn't enjoy getting my hands dirty or rolling in the mud. Cleaning off the grill was a dirty business, and I preferred the quizzical looks from my guests as I donned a pair of gloves to getting burnt fat lodged under my fingernails.

The warm morning had turned into a hot afternoon and I was grateful for the bit of shade provided by the tattered green canopy on my patio. I kept the gloves on until I had carefully arranged the charcoal into multiple small clusters, each one with a space left in the middle to accommodate a chunk of solidified kerosene that would gradually ignite the coals.

It is customary at a South African braai (and, I believe, at most barbeques in other parts of the world too) for the men to congregate outside, beers in hand. One of their number (often, but not necessarily, the host) is nominated by the rest of the pack to assume the official title of Fire-tender and Meat-turner. He is recognisable by the pair of tongs that never leaves his hand and, occasionally, an apron. Depending on the climate, he and other members of the group may be shirtless, and they can often be expected to be wearing sandals and shorts.

Members of the pack will take turns sharing tales of their prowess at manly pursuits such as fishing, watching sports, or being hung over. Often, they will burst into raucous laughter, slapping one another on the back or playfully punching one another's arm. The occasional audible burp or bout of flatulence is not only accepted, but celebrated. From time to time, one will begin gesticulating wildly with his hands, trying to catch the attention of someone inside the house. This will usually occur when the bottle each member clutches so dearly starts to run dry. If he fails to flag down anyone within, he must undertake a pilgrimage to the fridge. His return is inevitably met by much whistling and applause as he distributes bottles to the rest of the pack.

The women usually gather in the kitchen. Popular culture suggests that their entire time indoors is spent making the salad, but this is something of a misrepresentation, particularly when the salad has been bought pre-prepared. In this instance, the setting is unimportant – the kitchen just happens to be where they chat and joke and laugh in relative peace.

Interacting and trying to socialise with men had always taken a great deal of effort on my part. Sometimes I'd try to fit in with them, nodding my head when I thought it was appropriate, pretending to laugh at the jokes, paying careful attention to my body language. I'm sure I tried too hard at times, and that it must have been obvious to some observers. Invariably, I'd grow fatigued, and eventually I'd just withdraw from the interaction. I did not yet know what I was, but I certainly knew what I was not. I may have been thought of as aloof or unsociable, but it often felt more sustainable to stand on the sidelines.

I would normally drift off to wherever the women were conversing. Sharing recipes or sympathising about 'man problems' came much more naturally to me than trying to objectify women, enthuse over sports or engage in pissing contests with the men.

Stereotypical behaviours and tropes notwithstanding, I found myself fundamentally more comfortable in the company of women. I was less intimidated and less guarded. I found it easier to breathe and easier, even, to speak. There was a vague but unmistakable sensation of kinship and belonging that I had never experienced in the company of men.

I had just lit the kerosene cubes when the men emerged onto the patio. Zach was tall and gangly, though he'd put on some weight around the middle in recent months. His blonde hair was always long and untidy, and he had a way of looking sleepy even with his eyes wide open. Marcus was a little older, and a little more tanned than Zach – just as tall, much rounder and usually louder. He had a commanding physical presence, and he clearly enjoyed it.

The importance of the handshake had always been lost on me. It occupied a strange grey area between the wave that is appropriate for strangers and the hug that is reserved for closer friends or family members. Sometimes the handshake is a test of strength – we live in a society in which the strength of one's interosseous and lumbrical muscles is the most accurate measure of one's worth. Sometimes it's a socially acceptable, structured way for men to engage in physical contact – useful for those situations in which a hug may provoke an attack of homophobic panic, usually one's own.

The handshake always seemed like a silly ritual to me, not to mention an unsanitary one. Every time a hand was stretched out towards me, I wondered when last it had been washed, and I made a mental note to wash my own at my earliest convenience. As time passed, the custom became no longer inconvenient but painful – a stark reminder of how the world viewed me, and how that conflicted with my own sense of identity.

Zach and Marcus sequentially proffered their hands in greeting, as I knew they would. I swallowed hard, returning the gesture. Soon afterwards, I scurried inside under the pretence of returning the firelighters to their natural place in the cupboard under the sink. I washed my hands, then contrived to help prepare the ready-made salad.

Jennifer was engaged in pedestrian chit-chat with the others. I offered to freshen up the drinks for the group and topped up the snack bowls. I had always been the more attentive one when we had guests around. I didn't mind especially – it came naturally to me and, at the same time, taking on those responsibilities afforded me a convenient excuse to escape from uncomfortable or awkward situations, such as the one outside.

I don't know what was discussed on the patio that day. Cars, weapons, gadgetry and sex, perhaps. Maybe I underestimated the men, who may have been discussing the intersectional oppression of marginalised social groups.

Either way, the bits and pieces of it I'd catch when I'd briefly go outside to turn the meat didn't matter to me.

Cryobank

Day −149, 2 February 2015

The place had been easy enough to find, and the traffic not as heavy as I'd anticipated. I pulled up to the entrance of the office park with a good twenty minutes to spare.

'Where to?' asked the guard attending the gate.

'Cryobank,' I replied, adjusting my tie as nonchalantly as I could.

As he gave me directions and waved me through the gate, I couldn't help wondering if he knew to which sort of place I was headed, and what I was about to do there. There must have been fifteen companies with offices on the premises – I tried to convince myself that the guard didn't know what each one did and that, even if he did, he didn't care. Of course, I still couldn't shake the sensation of having all the eyes in the world fixed on me.

I have always been punctual – never late, probably early. But I've come to learn that arriving early is seldom a good thing. Idle minutes pass like hours, the ideal setting for dread to fester and fears to multiply. I never imagined myself likely to want children. The idea of parenthood had always seemed particularly abhorrent to me, probably as a result of my own less-than-idyllic childhood; with the world already overpopulated and in a generally miserable state, even if I did want children, adoption always seemed the more responsible – and, indeed, humane – approach. So, I began to wonder: why was I sitting in this parking lot, heart thumping, waiting with miserable anticipation for this wretched place to open its doors?

I knew the hormones would render me infertile in short order once I started taking them. The effects were theoretically reversible on cessation of therapy, a prospect I was not willing to entertain. This journey would last forever, which started to feel like an awfully long time when I thought about it. But, if nothing else, I was responsible, and this was the responsible thing to do. It was one of the more distasteful steps I'd have to take, but one from which I could not back away.

As I reached for the door handle, I took a moment to clear my mind. Then, with my best impersonation of a confident stride, I headed for the reception desk. I stammered a friendly greeting while the receptionist typed away at her computer. I wondered whether she'd heard me and was debating whether to repeat myself when, without so much as looking away from the screen, she answered me.

'What are you here for?'

'Cryopreservation,' I replied, as if it were the most normal answer in the world.

'How many days of abstinence?'

At least buy me dinner first, I thought. 'Four.'

She wrote the number down, ticked a few boxes and handed me the rest of the form to complete while she made the perfunctory but irrefutably necessary copies of my ID book, driver's licence, medical aid card and whichever other personal information Management had deemed appropriate.

After ensuring that I'd completed the form to her satisfaction, she stepped out from behind the desk and instructed me to follow her down a narrow corridor. At the end stood an unremarkable door, painted in the same humourless white as every other door we'd passed on the way.

'This is our Masturbation Room,' she said as she pushed the door open, revealing a small room with a washbasin in one corner, a small desk in the other, and an examination couch pressed up against the wall.

'There are videos on the computer. Sex videos,' she said. 'Return to the front when you are done.'

A tub of petroleum jelly sat on the washbasin. The desk was home to a computer monitor and a sticky-looking mouse. I examined the tub a little more closely and swore that I could see a hair sticking out from under the lid. I perched myself on the very edge of the examination bed, and began to undo my trousers under the cold white fluorescent light. I briefly considered making a run for the parking lot, but had spent the past week morbidly anticipating this encounter and would be damned if I was going to give up.

The small, cold room could best be described as counter-erotic; between the overused tub of lubricant and the equally overused computer, it was difficult not to wonder how many people had been here before me, and how thoroughly the room had been cleaned afterwards. But I didn't have a choice. Besides, this hardship was not likely to be the worst I'd have to face.

I relied on what little I knew about meditation to accomplish my objective. My hands shook as I secured the plastic container's ill-fitting red lid, overcome with fear and a bit of nausea at the thought of the slightest fumble sending the specimen plummeting to the floor. And I did not savour the thought of having to come back.

I washed my hands thoroughly, dried them off, cringed just a little, and then washed them again. I emerged from the Masturbation Room clutching my specimen tightly. The receptionist sat distracted, the surface of her desk only barely visible beneath the multitude of forms and other little plastic containers with red tops. She snatched the container from my hand; it joined its kin on her desk. I took a deep breath and hoped she'd written my name on the label. After grappling with her computer for a few minutes, the receptionist managed to print something that resembled an invoice. All that was left to do was pay the requisite fees and have some blood drawn for screening tests.

The phlebotomist looked as though he'd recently celebrated his 150th birthday but, to his credit, his hands were as steady as those of a spritely 120-year-old. After pricking me four or five times, he finally managed to pin down the elusive vein in the crook of my elbow.

51

The ordeal over at last, I climbed into my car and realised that I had enough time to stop in at home for a shower before going to work. I exfoliated even more vigorously than usual, trying to scrub off the indignity of the morning's proceedings.

It was about midday when an e-mail notification flashed onto my screen: the specimen was a little viscous, but the gametes were healthy and motile; the freeze was altogether successful; and 13 'straws' of genetic material were now in storage, hopefully correctly labelled.

You are, however, three straws short of the amount recommended to ensure a successful pregnancy. Do you think you'd be able to drop by and produce another specimen?

I tried not to think about it at all for the three days that followed.

Six more months

Day –142, 9 February 2015

'So – tell me *everything*,' said the endocrinologist as I settled into one of the two seats in front of her desk.

Dr Kim Williams was dressed in black leggings and a long, flowing orange top that I suspected was probably viscose. Her yellow wedges clashed perfectly with the rest of her outfit, and she wore multiple chunky bracelets that jangled with every wave of her arm. She was, of course, given to talking with her hands.

Before I'd even had a proper chance to speak, she was interrupting me: 'So you *want* to be a girl?'

*   *   *

When I'd first entered her office, I'd thought her somewhat eccentric. I knew that she managed hormone therapy for a number of patients who were transitioning, though her primary interests were diabetes and thyroid disorders. My psychiatrist seemed to trust her.

I'd arrived at the rooms early – Dr Williams's receptionist had made it very clear that I needed to be there half an hour before the scheduled time. I didn't ask why; the practice was obviously a busy one, and I was grateful to have been squeezed in at all.

After filling out the typical form, I was led through to a small examination room where Martha, the practice's rotund nurse, awaited me. She spoke loudly and slowly, explaining the series of short tests and examinations she was about to perform.

'Every time you come in to see doctor, we will start by testing your sugar and checking your blood pressure and examining your urine. Today we will do an ECG – a test for your heart. But only the first time, or if the doctor asks for it.'

She must have had the whole speech memorised, as she scarcely seemed to be paying attention as she recited the Litany of the New Patient. I was enjoying the theatrics enough that I decided not to risk jeopardising her performance by mentioning that I was a medical doctor myself.

She measured my blood pressure – I realised it was a little elevated, but according to Martha, it was very good. She asked why I had such a high heart rate, and I responded with an innocuous laugh, saying, 'Oh, I must just be a bit nervous, is all.'

Next was the ECG. She reached for a disposable razor and asked me to remove my pink polo shirt (selected by virtue of it being the most androgynous item of men's clothing I owned). She put the razor down silently as she realised my chest was already hairless, and she had the professionalism not to make any remarks about my navel piercing. She attached the 12 electrodes and told me to lie back and relax; within a few moments the machine noisily printed out a textbook cardiogram.

Martha left me to get dressed again, and I wandered back into the waiting room a few moments later. The seat I'd sat in before had a new occupant who must've arrived while I was in the examination room. I regarded her briefly with mild disdain and chose a different chair in a different corner, realising that having to change seats was likely to be the least traumatic part of the day's proceedings.

I had been cautioned that Dr Williams, despite her experience in managing patients with the medical aspects of their transition, may not, in fact, be quite so expert in the non-biochemical aspects of gender. I'd been advised to present in as androgynous a manner as possible, to shave before the appointment, and generally to act as 'queer' as I could manage. I was not very visibly queer, however, nor had I ever been. I knew how to present as male, having had a good few years of practice. I knew what society expected of me, and I was adept at playing that role. I knew how to present as female, because it came naturally to me. The body language, the gestures, the pattern of speech were behaviours that emerged easily as soon as I stopped trying to disguise them. Between male and female, there was not so much a grey area as a mysterious void – androgyny was an enigma to me, something I could see and appreciate in others, but which I never desired for myself.

I quickly dispensed with the notion of trying to present any sort of ambiguous appearance. I had discussed the idea with my therapist, and she had agreed with me – it would be better to be open and forthcoming, and try to make some sort of emotional connection with the doctor, than to try to play a role that I knew would be artificial and insincere. It is the endocrinologist's responsibility to handle the hormonal balance of the body, delicately and safely shifting the scales until the chemistry reaches a new equilibrium, one that aligns with the patient's identity and sense of self. It's not her job to diagnose the 'condition'.

* * *

So you want to be a girl?
I knew what the outcome of this consultation would be. It had become apparent that she knew little about gender outside of its hormonal aspects. Worse than that, I could tell that *she didn't know that she didn't know.*

I often used to say that I was not much of an activist. It would have been more accurate, in those days, for me to have said that I *was* an activist, but that my activism was quiet and non-confrontational. Had this not been so, I would undoubtedly have embarked on a tirade, carefully detailing to her the multitude of insensitivities that lay beneath her question.

Instead, I took a breath and resigned myself to the fact that this appointment was going to be altogether fruitless; my inner activist resolved to find a way, one day, to give patients in my position a better experience.

As she continued to question me about my history, it became quite obvious that Dr Williams had not even taken a cursory glance at the detailed report that my psychologist had prepared for her. Between her wild gesticulations and her rushed questions, she'd make mention of how she preferred her patients to have been in therapy for an arbitrary number of weeks or months or years before treating them. I believe she was doing what those in the business refer to as managing expectations.

She needn't have worried; I had already managed my own expectations. I'd made peace with the fact that Dr Williams was, for whatever reason, not going to be comfortable with treating me, and I knew that she wasn't my last resort. She lacked empathy and understanding, and no amount of her 'gut feeling' could make me second-guess what I'd known for so long to be true.

It's easy to say to someone, 'Come back after you've been in therapy for a further six months.' It didn't matter that my therapist had already concluded that my gender identity did not require any further therapy – I had it all figured out, and we'd spent recent weeks working on interpersonal relationships. More ironic was that she claimed to trust my psychologist implicitly, despite the two never having met in person, and despite Dr Williams not even having taken the time to read my psychologist's meticulously crafted reports.

She asked me why I hadn't self-medicated. Because, surely, if I was serious about this, I would have. Despite knowing the dangers and the risks. I had made a decision not to be irresponsible with this process, to undertake it safely and with the objective guidance of a qualified medical professional. To look after myself properly, because – for the first time in my life – I felt like I wanted to.

She conducted a routine physical examination, and pretended to take an interest in my own practice. She asked me if I didn't find it tedious treating snotty noses and stubbed toes, clearly of the opinion that endocrinology was a discipline far more noble than lowly general practice. I nudged back by telling her that I found it rewarding, because a general practitioner needed to know *everything*. She hid a scowl as she led me back to the office.

Her 'Come back in six months' seems an innocuous enough statement, at first glance. But what it means, in fact, is: 'Live with dysphoria for another six months. Another 180 days before we even *start* to initiate any changes that will make your body feel more like your own. That's 24 weeks spent knowing you could be taking action instead of waiting in pain.'

She said she'd consult with my psychologist and come back to me with an answer, though I already had no doubt about what that answer would be. She began suggesting steps I could take in the interim.

'You should start shopping for clothes.'

'I have a full wardrobe already.'

'You need to go and freeze sperm.'

'It's done. I was at the Cryobank twice last week.'

'Go for hair removal.'

'I've been waxing for the past eight months. I've been for three sessions of laser, and my next is coming up.'

'You should take a make-up course.'

'Honey, I could *teach* a make-up course. If *you* need any tips, feel free to ask.'

Eventually she realised that she could make no useful suggestions. Apparently, I was far less clueless about being a girl than she had assumed. She assured me once again that she'd give me a call later that afternoon, once she'd spoken to my psychologist.

As I walked out of her rooms, there was little doubt in my mind that Dr Williams didn't especially want to treat me. It worried me less than I may have imagined. Her feelings made me no less certain of who I was. Transition was my only recourse, and

57

pursue it I would; I was fortunate enough to have the resources to do so.

My life was not willing to be put on hold without adequate reason. It demanded to be lived. I wondered if, six months later, she'd be able to understand that.

Selfie-esteem

Day 9, 10 July 2015

I browse the shelves in the bookstore, scanning the titles, occasionally picking one up to page through. I am so engrossed that I startle a little when I feel a hand on my shoulder.

'Hello, you!' The voice is loud and exuberant.

I spin on my heel to see Edith standing behind me.

I knew her as a patient for a few years at the practice where I used to work. She had, on more than one occasion, proclaimed herself to be my favourite patient. I had many favourite patients, and Edith was no doubt amongst them.

'So good to see you!' I say, as I reach in to embrace her, settling from the initial surprise.

* * *

As far back as I could recall, I had always been camera-shy. Even as a child, I'd been reluctant to pose for photographs. I was self-conscious, stilted, ill at ease, never really able to relax in front of the lens, and always unimpressed with the results.

My body felt as though it just didn't fit, as though it betrayed me. I didn't understand why, of course. There is a surprising degree of social pressure to appear in photographs. Gatherings of friends or family often demand to be commemorated with group photographs. Some social media require photos of us to validate our online presence. Identity documents and driver's licences and passports all need photographs. A holiday is not a holiday unless we can produce, as evidence, photographs

59

of ourselves next to landmarks and monuments and local restaurants.

Living in the Instagram age was an uncomfortable existence for me.

My aversion to photographs became much easier for me to understand once I recognised where it originated. I remember poring over photos of myself, trying to find the features that upset me so. I was never able to. I saw no individual aspects to explain why I felt so distressed. It wasn't one single thing: it was everything. It only made sense once I understood how dysphoria worked. Photographs were dysphoria made manifest: they highlighted everything that was wrong with my body and put it on display. They were reminders of how everything failed to fit, of the constellation of physical features that were forever at odds with my identity. They made my struggle to claim ownership of my body official: I was disenfranchised, subjugated, stripped of my liberty. It was no wonder I had always hated them.

As I realised that transitioning was a necessity for me, I began, slowly, to set about reclaiming my body. I felt betrayed by its insistence on sprouting hair in inconvenient places, its predisposition to forming muscle, its unwillingness to grow soft, pleasing curves. The characteristics that it should have had were painfully absent, and those that it should have lacked were painfully present. Nonetheless, it was my body. If I were to continue living in it, I had to reclaim it and begin to reconcile it with my sense of self.

I needed to embrace my body, rather than punish it. I needed to nurture and support it, gently guiding it towards becoming what I wished it had always been. The time for resentment was over; I needed to learn how to start loving it instead.

How to start loving *her* instead.

Even before I began hormone therapy, the photograph had become a useful weapon in my battle against dysphoria. I began finding the few spare hours that I needed to take a few self-portraits in front of my tripod-mounted camera. I took hundreds of shots, carefully sifting through them afterwards and picking out the ones in which I looked best – the ones that drew attention to the physical characteristics that I found pleasing, and away from the characteristics that I disliked.

They served as evidence of the beauty inside me, especially in those inevitable times when my body image slumped, taking my self-esteem with it. They were proof of my identity, and they gave me reason to be optimistic. They reminded me that my body belonged to me, not I to it.

The photoshoot for which I modelled almost three months before taking my first dose of oestrogen had been a turning point of sorts. Toni, a close friend and professional photographer, had treated me like a beautiful model, and the opportunity to see myself through her lens helped me to understand that my beauty was objective, legitimate and true. That I had not been fooling myself. It allowed me the freedom, for a few hours, to cast off the guise that had always held me back. The graceful, elegant, glowing woman in those photographs had always lived within me, fighting for her freedom.

As time passed, photographs became my witness of how my body was changing – slowly, sometimes even imperceptibly. The redistribution of body fat, the softening of skin, the filling out of cheeks. Much of it was hard to notice, especially since I looked at myself daily in the mirror. Friends would remark about how my hips had grown, or my waist had narrowed, and I'd wonder if it were true, having failed to notice the changes myself. The photos were testament to those changes, proving to me just how diligently the hormones were working.

As I started to feel more at home in my body, my confidence grew. I no longer had to prepare myself for the ordeal of taking photos, and I often found myself in front of the mirror in a few spare moments before going out, snapping a quick few shots of myself with my mobile.

The difference was remarkable. I no longer hid from the camera. I became proud of my photos, understanding how powerful they were. They gave me agency over my body and control of my image. They reminded me of the good, whereas before they had only ever showcased the bad.

Somewhere along the way, I had rediscovered how to smile and found that it suited me.

I became more liberal with sharing the photos I took. I had taken to posting them on social media with some degree of regularity, often captioning them in ways that made it clear that I was proud not only of my appearance, but of my trans identity as well.

At first glance, it may have seemed conceited. But the photos were never a matter of vanity or narcissism. They were a form of expression, and they were statements. The images were parts of myself – my humanity, my honesty and, most of all, my vulnerability. They were testimony of the fight I had endured, and that I continued to endure, to claim ownership of my body.

They helped others to understand. The photos let them see for themselves that the disguise I'd worn before was just that – a misrepresentation. It allowed them to break the associations that they'd had in their minds, to let go of the concept of who I had pretended to be, and to see me at ease, relaxed, and happy in my truth.

The photos I shared always generated a positive response, which was empowering beyond words. The outpouring of support and encouragement took me by surprise. Seated at my computer, in pyjamas, my hair a mess, I'd log on to find the comments waiting for me:

'Gorgeous!'

'So beautiful!'

'Proud of you!'

'Congratulations!'

Even at home in pyjamas, I felt beautiful and radiant and authentic.

Every photo I shared was my way of saying, 'This is the woman that I am. The woman who has remained hidden for so long, but who has learnt, at last, to love herself.'

*　*　*

Edith had always been playfully antagonistic around me, and I imagine it had been her way of hiding that she was a little anxious or on edge. Today, there is no anxiety – just warmth, joy and affection.

We release each other, and she spends a moment looking me over, top to toe.

'You look gorgeous!' she says. 'So beautiful!'

I feel my cheeks start to flush, as she quickly adds, 'Even better than in your photos!'

I can't help smiling. Not that I mind; after all, it suits me.

Tablets

Day –142, 9 February 2015

In my university years, Emily had been one of my closest friends. We were both native to Johannesburg, but were studying in Pretoria. Geographically, the two were about fifty kilometres apart. Culturally, the distance was far greater. We bonded quickly over our shared experiences, almost like two expatriates discovering their commonality. We'd both had milkshakes as kids at the Doll House, one of Joburg's better-known roadhouses. We'd both been to see movies at Sandton City, we both remembered the flea market at Bruma Lake. And, as students, we both used to listen to Gareth Cliff making people angry while we sat bumper to bumper on the N1, trying to get to Pretoria in time for our classes

I hadn't seen Emily in more than a year. Previously, distance had been the complicating factor, but now something else always seemed to get in the way – work, or family commitments, or sometimes just laziness. I had never stopped caring for her, and I tried to make sure I vocalised that on the rare occasions that we did talk – usually on the phone on each other's birthdays.

The last time I'd seen her, she'd been a mother of two. Now, she was a mother of three, still nursing, and always busy. It was difficult to get hold of her on the phone, so instant messages would have to do.

> *Hey. I hope you're well! Miss you. I'd love to be able to talk soon, if you have a chance?*

The reply took a few days to come.

Sorry it's taken me so long to get back to you! What's going on?

I hadn't given away much up to that point, but Emily had always been intuitive about my feelings, even when I'd tried to guard them. She knew that whatever it was, it was serious.

I don't like to drop bombshells on my friends through instant message. I'd really prefer to do this face to face.

Uh uh! Just tell me, whatever it is!

I'd lost my will to argue, in any event.
I'm gender dysphoric, I typed, and my fingers trembled above the send button. I closed my eyes, breathed deeply, and heard the ping that told me my message had been delivered. *No going back now,* I thought, feeling relief.
The reply came even sooner than I had expected.

I think I knew that, my friend ...

She didn't want to discuss it any further until we could meet, a sentiment with which I agreed. We arranged to meet up the next afternoon, after my appointment with the endocrinologist. I offered to make the trip to Pretoria; I knew it wouldn't be easy for her to travel far from home, and I had been desperate to see her again, for the first time with this weight lifted off my shoulders.
The highway was, fortunately, as painless as it should've been in the middle of the day. I knew the road well enough, having travelled it back and forth almost every day for the better part of six years while I was a student. I found my way to the small café she had chosen – it was in a very small shopping centre, close enough to the main road to be accessible but far away enough for the noise not to travel.

It was a trendy, whole-food, vegan-friendly, eco-conscious, organic coffee shop. I knew before I'd even sat down that they would have wheatgrass on the menu, and probably more than one variety. The interior was cluttered with organic spreads, lactose-free snacks and a variety of fair-trade oils, stacked high on industrial-style shelves set against a plain screed floor. Less is more, as they say.

Emily was already seated when I arrived, at an outside table in the shade. She looked a little tired, but she hadn't changed from university days – her tanned, almost olive complexion, and her dark hair that she insisted on straightening. She wore a pale orange summer dress and sandals. As ever, her voice was lilting and melodic. Her face broke into a wide smile when she saw me and we embraced more tightly than I'd remembered us doing in the past. She'd always had a calming effect on me, and that hadn't changed either. I'd already put the morning's events behind me, but was still somewhat on edge. I wondered if she heard my sigh of relief as we hugged.

We spent a few minutes exchanging pleasantries. I asked after her children, and her husband, and her job at the psychiatric hospital. She asked about my break-up, and my mom, and my brother. She told me that she'd suspected that something was different about me for a long time. It was the lack of sexual tension between us, despite our closeness, that had first tipped her off. She had always found me easy to relate to, and she'd always been comfortable around me. She couldn't put her finger on what it was, but she'd guessed that I was probably gay. Hearing that I was transgender didn't come as much of a shock to her.

Despite the fact that she was studying psychiatry as a post-graduate, she was still a little unsure of the implications. She had a good few questions, starting – as so many people do – with my sexuality.

'So, do you like boys, then?' Emily asked.

I sighed, and drew my breath, before I patiently explained that sexual orientation and gender identity were not dependent on each other. I detailed to her how I'd never felt like I fitted in with other boys, how it was easier to relate to women, how I always felt I had society's eyes on me.

She asked if I planned to live 'on the other side', and I explained to her that I didn't have a choice. To carry on pretending would be unnatural, even abhorrent. She grappled with the concept as she tried to understand. I took out my phone and found a photo of me from a shoot I'd done at the end of December. Her first reaction was, 'You look *so* happy.'

We chatted a bit about make-up and shoes. She told me she worried I may grow breasts bigger than hers. Time passed quickly, and soon she had to leave so that she could be home to feed her youngest. I stayed behind and settled the bill, smiling to the waitress and wishing her a good afternoon as I left.

I drove home patiently, feeling relaxed and at ease. It had been good to see Emily again after so long. She was still optimistic, friendly, soft-spoken and just a little naïve. I knew she had only my best interests at heart. She phoned me later in the evening to tell me that she wanted me to be happy, but she worried about whether I'd find acceptance in the world.

'Are you sure?' she'd asked.

'I've thought about it,' I answered, 'I promise you.'

'I'm just worried about you. What will people say? What will they think of you?'

It stung a little, this reminder of the prejudice that lurks deep within people's hearts and minds. And though I appreciated that her concern was good-natured, I struggled for a moment or two as I realised that Emily may still have thought that there was some decision to be made.

I composed myself quickly.

'It doesn't matter what they think,' I said. 'I have to do this if I'm going to survive. I appreciate your concern, and I know you mean well, but this is something I have to do. There is adversity lying in wait, no matter which path we take. It's something that needs to be faced, rather than avoided.'

I could hear by her voice that she was still concerned, but she knew that I wasn't going to change course – I couldn't. I explained to her as best I could that I had no choice in the matter. To continue living as I had been was not to live at all.

On the drive home from our lunch, I decided that it was time to stop gazing wistfully at the boxes of tablets that had sat untouched in my cupboard for the past 12 days. When our conversation ended, I calmly opened them and extracted a tablet from each. I laid them out on my palm, and looked at them for a moment. I placed them on my tongue and swallowed them.

For such a significant step, the whole thing felt anticlimactic. I didn't mind that at all.

Gender issues

Day –139, 12 February 2015

The phone call must have surprised my mother. It was unchar-
acteristic of me, to say the least, to invite her to join me for
lunch. I had been avoiding her; she knew it, and I knew that she
knew it. It had been this way for years. It hurt me, and I was
sure that it hurt her, but it was easier to keep her at a distance
than to try to let her back in after so much time had passed. I
knew I had to tell her the truth about myself, and soon.

I hadn't picked a time or a date, but I wanted it to be before
my body changed in any noticeable way – I felt I owed her that
much. Every so often, I'd have a particularly slow day at work.
I could not predict when they were going to happen, nor could
I determine why. Perhaps sometimes the universe just gave
people a day off from being sick.

It was one of those quiet days. I left the rooms early. I had a
few errands to attend to, but it was the first afternoon I'd had
free in what felt like months. I'd become used to spending these
afternoons with doctors, or psychologists, or laser-hair-removal
therapists. I was exhausted, and although the idea of returning
home for an afternoon nap was incredibly appealing, I knew
that this was my best opportunity for what I knew was going to
be a difficult conversation.

I could feel the nervousness rising from the pit of my stomach,
that feeling of foreboding that so often precedes defining moments
in our lives. My mother and I had arranged that I would meet
her at her townhouse, and we'd go together to the mall.

I headed down Johannesburg Road, the route to her home all
too familiar. I reminisced as I drove, remembering scattered

scenes from my childhood: the toy store behind the Spar, the small café that used to sell fancy imported sweets that couldn't be found elsewhere, the boys-only high school from which we used to fetch my older brother Leo most afternoons. The toy store had been replaced by a laundromat, and the café was now a micro-lender and a hair salon. The high school still stood, but half the sports field had been dug up.

Before long, I arrived at the townhouse. I rang the bell, and my mother appeared to greet me. She was dressed in sweatpants and sneakers, and a baggy pink top. Her hair was curly, but its once vivid auburn had long given way to grey. We exchanged greetings and headed off towards the nearby mall.

She drove; I sat uncomfortably in the passenger seat. She insisted on putting in petrol before anything else. It reminded me of the countless times she'd stopped for petrol with me in the car as a child. I'd always thought of her as being a little peculiar in that sense – she had a favourite service station, to which she insisted on going even if it was out of the way. The staff there had been languid; each time I'd point out to her how ridiculously slow it had been. She'd agree with me wholeheartedly, and fill up at the same service station the next time around.

This occasion was no less frustrating – she spent a good five minutes deliberating over which credit card she wanted to use. To me, it seemed like a simple decision, but to her it was obviously one of great importance. After a few moments' consideration, I determined that I lacked the insight to appreciate its significance.

Finally, we left the petrol station and arrived at Eastgate. She deliberated again over where exactly she wanted to park, while I tried not to let my mounting frustration show. At last, we made it to the food court, and she chose a restaurant that seemed to her to be sufficiently airy and quiet. She was concerned about the heat, and asked the waitress at least three times which was cooler – the indoor or outdoor seating areas. She eventually decided that it would be best to sit in the doorway between the two, to benefit from both the gentle breeze outside and the air conditioning within.

Lunch was disappointing on many levels. The food was bland and meagre, the service inattentive, and the conversation dismal. I struggled to maintain eye contact with her for more than a few seconds at a time. I couldn't keep my hands still, and was relieved when my phone rang as it granted me a brief respite from our strained interaction.

I was becoming frustrated and tired, and a headache that had originally been just a mild and dull pain threatened to overwhelm me. I was wavering, the prospect of escape quickly becoming more important to me than the prospect of disclosing to my mother what I'd been going through.

I determined that the best course of action was to try to survive this tedious outing, and reassess my position once we were back at her home. The bill finally settled, I was just a few minutes away from being able to abort my misguided plan. I may even be able to fit a short nap into what remained of this miserable afternoon.

She parked in the driveway. I stood waiting to say goodbye and bolt for my own car, but she insisted I come inside to fetch the mail she'd been collecting for me since the last time we met. Post in hand, I made a turn for the door, disappointed. The rational choice would have been to cut my losses and gather my strength to try again another day. I'd be more careful in selecting a venue for the meeting, I'd make sure I was well rested, I'd get the words out before she had a chance to annoy and frustrate and nag me. Or maybe I'd avoid it altogether – just write her a letter and allow her to make the next move.

My hand must've been almost on the door handle when I turned back.

'I've been in therapy for a few weeks.'

My voice was softer as I spoke the words than I'd expected it to be. It was an announcement, albeit a meek one.

'That must have been a big step for you,' she acknowledged.

I realised that she'd assumed, and reasonably so, that I'd been seeing a psychologist to deal with the emotional abuse I had suffered as a child. I'd made it this far – I just needed to find the words.

'The reason I'm in therapy,' I stammered, 'is that I'm having gender issues.'

I couldn't bring myself to be any more specific. Even phrased like that, my heart thumped in my chest and my mouth grew dry. Eye contact was out of the question.

She was silent for a moment or two.

'Gender issues?' she echoed.

She had a few questions, some more insightful than others.

'Couldn't you rather just have been gay?' my mother asked, only half joking.

'It's not quite that simple,' I replied.

I made an effort to be patient, to answer her questions as comprehensively as I could, and not to skimp on the details as she'd accused me of doing so many times before.

I knew she didn't understand all the intricacies and implications of what I'd told her. I didn't want to bog her down with details when I knew she would struggle to process the few she had.

We parted with an awkward, quick embrace.

I came home feeling tender and vulnerable. I spent a good half an hour standing under a hot shower, shaving everything and trying to scrub off the remains of the day. A good all-over shave always left me feeling settled and more comfortable, sensations I direly needed.

Sleep came easily, and I was thankful for it.

When I awoke, an e-mail was waiting for me.

Hi A

Thanks for lunch and sharing your rather 'devastating' news. I'm heartbroken that you've gone through your whole life so far feeling that you had to keep it all to yourself. I will support you however I can so please don't alienate

me as you have done these past three years. I might get on
your nerves at times but remember that's what mothers
do! Nothing is insurmountable and you don't have to do
it alone.
I love you lots, my very special precious child.
Mum xxxxx

It would take her a while, I realised, to break the habit of using
my deadname, and to start getting my pronouns right – a detail
that seemed trivial in that instant as I wiped away the tears
that had formed while I was reading.

Like the patriarchy

Day −448, 9 April 2014

Jennifer lay sprawled on her back, her tanned skin contrasting starkly with the soft, white sheets. I ran my fingers through her raven hair, gently tracing her scalp as I nibbled on her ear. I worked my way down her neck, caressing her with my tongue as the tips of my fingers found their way beneath her bra straps. I continued to nuzzle and peck, lingering on her collarbones as I unfastened the garment. She was eager to throw it off, but I stopped her, wanting to savour each moment, each inch of soft flesh as it was laid bare before me. I wanted to taste and kiss every valley, every ridge, every pore, patiently allowing the tension to build.

*   *   *

Jennifer and I had been a couple for over seven years. We'd met in medical school, where we'd both felt like outcasts. She was Buddhist, and I was Jewish, and we were studying in very conservative Pretoria. Hardly a day would go by when someone on campus would not proselytise one or both of us, hoping to 'save' us. Religious and personal freedom seemed a foreign concept to some of our classmates, and it was not surprising that she and I had found commonality.

We became good friends and, before too long, lovers. I'd been a shy virgin when I met her, innocent and naïve. She was inexperienced, but to a far lesser degree than I had been. Initially, I'd been scared of sex. Society conditions us to regard intercourse as some sort of Holy Grail, a universal goal for everyone, and for men even more so. I had always found the idea of sex intimidating and overwhelming and, sometimes, even a little repulsive. The very notion of allowing another human being such intimate access to my body and my emotions made me more than a little queasy.

Jennifer was impassioned and lustful, and she made it quite clear that she desired me physically as well as emotionally. I had grown to feel comfortable around her, and I was convinced that I was ready to face my fears and aversions. I felt safe and I was sure she would take care of me. The first time we'd been intimate, we'd arranged to spend a night at a bed and breakfast just outside of town. I'd been far less nervous than I had expected. The experience had been pleasant enough, though I remember being very concerned about the possibility that I may hurt her. Many years later, only after the two of us had broken up, she would tell me that she had caught a glimpse of me from behind that night, as I had risen in the middle of the night and walked to the bathroom. She had almost mistaken me for a woman.

Over the years, our relationship had endured more than its fair share of hardship: disapproving parents, the rigours of medical school, living in rural areas near to the hospitals at which government regulations had forced us to work. It had never been an easy journey for us, but we had survived. We'd often remark to each other how different our dynamic had been from those we saw in the relationships of our friends. It had been difficult, at the time, to pinpoint exactly what made us so different, but in retrospect, it seems obvious.

In our relationship, gender had been left at the door.

Ours had been a bond between two human beings, not between chromosomes or gonads or stereotypical embodiments of gender and gender roles. We'd each seen the other simply as people. We'd split the household chores, had each picked up the other's slack, and had taken it in turns to look after each other on the occasion that we'd taken ill. We'd both been uncomfortable, consciously or subconsciously, with the expectations that gender brought with it.

She'd worried that I would expect her to take care of all the cooking and cleaning and washing and ironing. And I'd been uncomfortable with the idea of having to be the 'man of the house', making all the decisions without her input, ordering her around and changing the occasional light bulb.

We'd aimed for a fair division of household responsibilities and, for the most part, we'd achieved it. She'd shop, I'd cook. I'd wash, she'd dry. One week I'd iron, the next she would. Any decisions that had needed to be made, we'd made together. Every time we'd gone out to a restaurant, I'd shrink uncomfortably when the host or the waiter had spoken to me and ignored her. At social gatherings, where the couples would often split up – the men at one end of the table and the women at the other – we'd remain in each other's company.

In a society consumed by gender, our relationship had been the one safe place to which I could escape. It was a place where the preconceptions and prejudices, and the expectations that did not fit, could no longer reach me. Where I'd not had to apologise for what I was not, and had felt no pressure to think about what I actually was.

I often wondered whether I would have been faced with the realisation of my gender identity sooner had it not been for that relationship.

Sex had always challenged us, however. When it came to intercourse, I had never been very good at imitating a man. I had always seen penetration as a poor excuse for lovemaking, and had been more interested in the intricacies of foreplay, the heightening of sensations and the building of desire. And I'd preferred to give than to receive, particularly when it came to oral stimulation. I'd found the act of giving oral sex to be intensely arousing and rewarding, though I'd enjoyed myself markedly less as the recipient.

Later, I would understand that Jennifer had struggled to please me, not just because of my base level of discomfort with my own body, but also because she had played with me as she would with a man. She'd try to stimulate me quickly and firmly, and she'd be surprised when it only left me annoyed and unhappy. I had always favoured a light touch, patient and tender, building slowly to a crescendo. I realised that at the time, I should have told her to pretend it was a clitoris rather than a cock. I felt guilty that she may have felt like she'd failed when, in my mind, the barriers to our sexual connection had all stemmed from my own body.

She'd often desired to be penetrated and, on occasion, I'd done my best to oblige, though it had taken a significant degree of concentration and focus on my part and had been unusual for me to climax in that way, much to her dismay. I'd endeavoured to thrust and push and pull and do all the things that I imagined I should have been doing. Sometimes, albeit quite infrequently, I'd be sufficiently aroused to be overcome with desire for her. In these moments, I did not feel the 'manliness' inherent in penetrative sex – I was just one human being making love to another. But for the most part, I'd tried to avoid these kinds of encounters with her. They'd been uncomfortable in so many ways, and had left me feeling ill at ease.

If there was a mirror next to the bed, I'd try to avoid it, and I'd keep my clothes on for as long as I possibly could. Often, I'd keep my eyes closed altogether. Even in her exclusive company, I'd been self-conscious and uncomfortable, particularly in the context of sex – many years before I would understand the reasons behind it all. I knew that Jennifer realised I was uncomfortable with sex, particularly in the traditional sense of the act, but we had never discussed why. I doubt that she ever truly understood until well after our relationship had ended.

I'd never been infatuated with my own genitalia in the way that people who possess such organs are supposed to be. The appendage itself had never struck me as being particularly attractive, or even all that well designed. It was in the way when flaccid, and especially in the way when not. Jennifer had often desired to lavish attention on it. Invariably, the muscles of my thighs would tense up, and I'd try to pull away. It had always been difficult for me to relax when her touch had wandered anywhere close to my crotch. I realised that I was fortunate that it had never consciously caused me significant or tremendous distress. The organ itself was not entirely abhorrent, but I would have been far more comfortable had there been a vulva in its place. I had always been happier letting it just be ignored. Later, I'd take to keeping it free of hair, and referring to it as 'she' in an effort to mitigate my no-longer-subconscious ill feelings for her.

* * *

77

I kissed my way down Jennifer's chest, slowly climbing her small but supple breasts and pausing just before I reached her nipple. She let out a soft moan as I caressed her, grazing her soft skin ever so gently with the edge of my nail. I held my mouth over her, close enough that I knew she'd feel my breath, as I lightly flicked my tongue across the soft surface of her breast. I locked my lips around her nipple and kissed her passionately as she writhed, all the while my hands inching further downward, tickling and stroking and charting the topology of her waist and her navel.

My lips brushed softly and gently against her, a flicker of tongue or a flash of teeth to surprise her every so often. My hands found their way to the waistband of her panties, reaching around the small of her back until they loosely cupped her buttocks. She rocked her hips back and forth, willing me ever closer to her, and pressed her palms against my head. Casually, I tugged on the elastic waistband, letting it snap against her hip as I released it. I looked up at her playfully, seeing the frustration mount in her eyes.

I freed her panties from around her hips, and traced along the outside of her thighs as I removed them, holding my face just inches from her crotch. The scent of her was unmistakable, wet and salty and wanton in desire. I resisted the temptation, holding myself back so I could explore her silky thighs. Her moans became louder as I finally reached her lips, by now slick and slippery. I found her clit, and licked around it. Slowly, deliberately, methodically. She writhed and she rocked and she moaned as I flicked my tongue across her, dawdling and lingering as I watched her excitement grow. Unhurriedly, I brought her to the edge, as I had countless times before. I felt her as her calves tightened, her fingers clenched against the sheets, her neck arched back and her hips thrust forward as her body was overtaken by spasms, her breath growing ever faster.

The moments drew out, feeling like hours, as she pressed her hips more closely to my lips, silently screaming with pleasure. She sank into the bed, struggling to catch her breath, her eyes beginning to glaze over as her heart began to settle; she clutched my hand firmly in hers, giving it a little squeeze.

'That was wonderful,' she sighed, 'but do you know what I'd really like one day?'

'Do tell,' I said.

'I'd like it if you could just fuck me. Really just fuck me, you know? Fuck me like the patriarchy.'

I rolled my eyes under the cover of darkness.

'I'll try,' I lied to her as she drifted off to sleep.

Tears

Day –124, 27 February 2015

I sat on the purple couch in front of the coffee table in my mother's living room. It had been our third encounter in as many weeks, and we'd talked on the phone on most of the intervening days. Before, we used to go for months without seeing each other. I felt guilty about maintaining that distance between us, but it had been the easiest recourse for me. I used to tell myself that it was okay to sweep the pain under the rug until I was ready to face it.

But now, our dynamic had changed, and drastically so. I found that it had become easier to talk to my mother, and I was more patient and more forthcoming and much less guarded. Of course, there was still some apprehension on both sides. Neither of us had any doubt that our relationship was moving in the right direction, but it was still so unfamiliar, and each of us was scared of making a misstep in these early days.

My mother had done some reading. I'd found a book for her that, despite being a little dated, did a fairly good job of explaining concepts and terminology like transition and gender dysphoria. Now that she had a little more information and insight, she wanted to see me in person to discuss what I was going through.

I had made myself scarce around what little extended family I had, in recent months. My aunt would sporadically extend invitations to me to join her and her family and, often, my mother for a Shabbos dinner or a Jewish holiday. My aunt has always been empathic and loving to family and strangers alike. Her Shabbos table was often an interesting and eclectic mix of personalities – one week, there'd be an Afrikaans couple who had converted to Judaism, the next there would be visitors from Ethiopia or Yemen or Tibet. Everyone was made to feel welcome, and no one left with an empty stomach.

There had been a few reasons for my absence lately. My recent break-up had been weighing on me, and I didn't always feel like company. Or I didn't feel that I would be good company. Fridays were the days I usually saw my therapist, and sometimes those encounters left me a little fragile. Occasionally, I just had prior commitments – dinners with friends, or a movie night or a party.

I'd taken, recently, to saying that I was in a 'funny place' about religion, which was a good way of saying that I no longer felt comfortable rationalising the misogyny and intolerance that permeated its dogma. My relationship with religion had always been strained – I had attended an Orthodox school, excelled at religious studies and imagined that I felt what was best described as a connection to the community. My parents, however, had never been religious and weren't especially enthusiastic about the prospect of their child becoming observant.

In the years in which I had lived independently, I had been geographically isolated from the Jewish community – matters of faith had been personal then, and I was happy with that. But since moving back to Johannesburg, I'd had to start thinking quite seriously about where I stood with regard to Judaism. Perhaps being trans made it easier: religion did not really know what to do with me. I was an outsider, best left alone. The feeling had started to become mutual.

I seldom spoke with my aunt on the phone – she'd usually just send a text message. It was obvious from her tone that she was concerned about me and would dearly like for me to accept one of her invitations. I'd given it a good deal of thought, and decided to take one for the team. I put on the single suit that I owned, paired with the nicest white double-cuffed shirt in my cupboard. A tie around my neck, cufflinks on my wrists and shiny black dress shoes, and I was ready to go. I did my best not to look at myself in the mirror on my way out. I may have looked the part, but certainly did not feel it.

I can be quite the conversationalist at times, but that evening I spent sitting quietly and contemplatively in my assigned seat. I politely ate soup and salad and meat and vegetables. I laughed and kept quiet when it was appropriate to do so, and tried not to let my discomfort show. I was inconspicuous and unremarkable, but I was *there*, and I hoped that would be enough.

By the end of the evening, I was fatigued, but my mother insisted that I accompany her back to her home so we could talk. I could still remember when she disposed of the old lounge suite she used to own and replaced it with the purple one. It must've been more than a decade ago, but in my mind, the couches were still new. It reminded me how easy it is not to notice as time passes. My mother was sixty-eight years old. I did my best not to realise it, but it still came as a shock when I did.

The coffee had finished brewing, and I poured a cup for myself. I was relieved that she'd had something other than decaf in the cupboard. It was good coffee – Illy, a brand renowned as much for its quality as for its price. There was another sealed tin of the same coffee in her cupboard. She tried to give it to me, but I refused – I told her to keep it so there'd be something for me to drink the next time I visited.

I had reciprocated her gesture with one of my own.

Each time we met or spoke seemed a little easier than the last. I still expected a barrage of questions, but it was not forthcoming. I thought there may have been something specific weighing on her mind, but I realised that there wasn't. She asked if it had been difficult for me to sit at my aunt's table. The truth was that it had been much harder than it used to be, but it had been the right thing to do.

We talked about my childhood: how her divorce from my father had affected me, and how he had manipulated me and bullied her into having me live with him. How he had made me feel guilty for having her as my mother and Leo as my brother. How I'd been torn between keeping the peace at home and trying to maintain relationships with the rest of my family. How I grew up relying on myself for emotional support, and how that had made it difficult for me to share my feelings.

I admitted to her that I had pushed her away and kept her at a distance, sometimes unwittingly, sometimes deliberately. I told her that when I'd finally worked up the nerve to tell her about my break-up, I'd had to put the phone down in the middle of the conversation because I didn't want her to hear me crying. I told her that I knew she felt guilty for what had happened to me, and to my relationship with her. I told her that I never wanted her to see me hurt or broken for fear that it may worsen the guilt she carried. That I didn't blame her, and held no resentment, and that for so long I had wanted things to be better between us but I didn't know how to change them.

As my mother put her arms around me, I cried in front of her for the first time in almost twenty years.

Coming out

Day –117, 6 March 2015

I had never liked the term 'coming out'. I wasn't quite sure why – it just didn't sit very well with me. Perhaps it's the implication that 'in' and 'out' are antithetical and mutually exclusive when, in fact, they lie on a spectrum. Maybe it's the idea that before one 'comes out', one engages knowingly in subterfuge and deception.

It could be that the term has come to be used so loosely and liberally – in this day and age, one can 'come out' as vegan, or libertarian, or as a lover of One Direction. The reality of coming out as transgender is infinitely more intimidating, its consequences more terrifying.

Despite my misgivings about the term, I realised that I had done a fair bit of coming out over the past few months. I did not have many close friends or family members, but had disclosed my gender identity to the majority of them. My mother knew and had, with my permission, told my aunt. My ex had known for a long time already. I'd told Emily. I was desperately awaiting an opportunity to tell my brother, Leo, who had always been a pillar of support, even when our relationship had become distant. All that held me back was geography – he lived a good fifteen hundred kilometres away, and I had resolved to tell him in person.

Disclosure was complicated. I had already come to terms with my gender identity – bits and pieces from my childhood and adolescence had fallen into place, and I could explain behaviours, emotions and sensations that I'd struggled to understand before. I'd spent countless hours figuring out how best to proceed on the journey that I knew I had to take. My realisation had been a gradual one. There'd been no single moment in which I'd known with blinding certainty what I had doubted before.

At various points in my life, I'd found myself acting as a support structure for my close friends when they had been through times of crisis. They had trusted me, sharing intimate personal details with me and looking to me for encouragement or advice or just a safe place. But many of those relationships had been one-sided: I had always felt compelled to be self-sufficient, and had never wanted to burden anyone with my own problems. I'd be quick to deflect personal questions with a joke or a quip, distracting my friends until they forgot the question or realised that I was uncomfortable answering it.

Even when my relationship with Jennifer came to an abrupt end, I had found solace in myself. It must've been a good month before I'd shared the information with friends or family. I had waited until the pain had subsided to the point of being manageable, until I had been able to put on a brave face and talk about it as if it were historical fact rather than personal experience.

I became so adept at misdirection that, for a time, I even managed to misdirect myself. I knew I was uncomfortable allowing anyone in, but I had not admitted the reasons why. On some level, I was aware that if I didn't let anyone get too close, people may pass me off as being a little odd or a bit different, but would think nothing more of it. But once I acknowledged the disparity between my gender and my sex, I immediately understood why I'd been so compelled to maintain such distance in many of my interactions. And I knew that my relationships and friendships had been founded on pretence. It was time to set that straight, to admit to the people I cared about who I really was and to try to rebuild those relationships – if people would allow me to do so.

I had to remember that although I'd had time to understand, those to whom I'd be disclosing would not have had that luxury. The revelation was always going to be a bombshell. There is no reliable way to soften such a blow, one that fundamentally alters the basis on which a relationship has been built.

Some people react with confusion, struggling to understand the words and their implications. Some react with anger, feeling that they've been deceived or manipulated. Some react with sorrow, overcome with a sense of loss that the person they once knew and loved is no more. Sometimes they are numb, as shock crashes over them like a tidal wave. Others wrap their arms around you and pull you closer, and tell you that everything is okay, that they already knew, or that they love you anyway. There's no way to predict it.

Coming out is an art, not a science. It's a careful balance of empathy, consideration and hope that you will not be rejected. It's faith that you will be met with acceptance and compassion. It's trust that even such life-changing shocks will become easier with time. And it's consolation that anyone who does not want to understand was not worth knowing in the first place.

The fear never goes away. The moment before you utter the words is a precipice, at the edge of which you summon all your courage and strength and resolve.

And then you jump.

'I am transgender.'

'...'

The silence can be deafening as you wait for a response that takes an eternity to arrive. But even before the answer comes the relief: the veil has been lifted. And part of you just wants to shout it out to the entire world, your glorious, challenging, terrifying truth.

A mental association thing

Day –113, 10 March 2015

Nick and I had been friends for about two years. When we met, he had owned a restaurant in Johannesburg, not far from where I lived. It had been easy to drop in from time to time for a quick chat. I'd never had many male friends. Nick proved to be a challenge for me too, though he was smart and affable.

He was ever so slightly taller than me, and a few years older. He'd worked in IT before becoming a restaurateur. He was heavy-set, and always wore a goatee. If you looked closely enough, you'd be able to spot a thick gold chain among the coarse chest hair that poked out from his trademark golf shirt.

Jennifer and I had become accustomed to dinner meetings with Nick and his fiancée Sofia when we were still a couple. Nick was quite the foodie, and was always seeking out new culinary hotspots. He was also something of a wine aficionado, much to teetotal Sofia's chagrin. She was an old-fashioned woman who believed in hard work. She had little time for frivolity, and she wouldn't hesitate to voice her disapproval when Nick tried to engage in any.

During these dinners, Nick would often try to involve Jennifer and me in lengthy discourse, usually on the subject of science fiction, or board games, or Magic: The Gathering. Sofia would sit tapping inattentively at her iPhone, while I would try in vain to change the subject to something more inclusive.

Nick was always easy to talk to, mostly because he'd happily carry an entire conversation on his own; all one had to do was feign attention and give the occasional nod. Sofia was easier to talk to because I could understand her, to a degree. She was even fussier when it came to what she would and wouldn't eat than I was. We both avoided alcohol, and generally preferred to stay in than go out. Her political views were far more conservative than mine, however.

The two had moved to Pretoria a few months earlier, where they'd opened a new restaurant that consumed much of their time. They had little opportunity to socialise as we had before, and the fifty-kilometre drive that now separated us had not made things any easier. Nick and I spoke on the phone every few weeks, each conversation typically ending with our vowing to make a plan to meet up in person soon.

We finally got around to setting a date for the long-overdue dinner. It was a Tuesday evening. Nick had sent me a message to tell me that Sofia would be joining us, if that was okay with me. I enjoyed Sofia's company, but I mentioned to him that there was a rather important conversation that I'd hoped to have with him in private. He pushed me to give him the details in a text message – he was worried it may be something catastrophic.

I'm gender dysphoric. See? No big deal.

Like Kris Jenner?

Bruce. And kind of. But that story has been distorted by the media.

I think they focus on a lot of the newbie facts and that's all.

Anyway … it's something I have been dealing with my whole life, though it took me a good deal of time to understand what it was.

Fair enough, something like this probably takes a while to put together and for you to know yourself. Are we still meeting up tonight? I am thinking Indian.

It was typical Nick: he was a *boytjie* through and through, carrying on as if nothing had happened, stoic and manly and unfazed.

We met at the fancy restaurant he'd selected (which turned
out not to be Indian, after he'd changed his mind at the last
minute), and the three of us endured a rather disappointing
dinner. I didn't know if he'd told Sofia, but neither of them
broached the subject. It had started to feel a little like the
elephant in the room. I did my best to ignore it.

We said our goodbyes, and went our respective ways. An hour
or so later, I sent another message.

*Are we cool? I can understand you might have some
processing to do. Take your time. If you have questions,
feel free.*

*Very cool. I don't need any processing here. It doesn't
change our friendship one bit.*

I appreciated the sentiment and tried not to feel invalidated,
reminding myself that despite what he said, he *did* need time
to process it. Everyone did.

The next day, he told me that Sofia had some questions. She
wanted to know how I knew. And she wanted to know about my
sexuality. I was surprised that hadn't been the first question.
They asked me if it was 'a state of mind' or 'a mental associa-
tion thing'. I didn't understand what either of those terms was
supposed to mean, but I was certain they were inaccurate. I
explained that it was my identity and my sense of self; the way
that I interacted with the world, and it with me. I explained
the term 'dysphoria', and the concept of feeling uncomfortable
in my own body. It was difficult to get my point across, but my
monster-under-the-bed analogy seemed to help.

*   *   *

It had been a week since I'd come out. I sat alone at the restaurant, waiting for Nick and Sofia to arrive. It was unlike them to be late, and it was already fifteen minutes later than the time we'd agreed on. They'd told me when we'd made the plan that their phones were low on battery, so I was not surprised when my calls went straight to voicemail. Insecurity took hold; I started to wonder whether I was being stood up.

A few minutes later, my phone rang. They were on their way. This time it was, in fact, an Indian restaurant, on a street corner in bustling Norwood. Restaurant-goers walked up and down the busy streets, as did salesmen trying to peddle wire sculptures. I sat at an outside table, the evening not being too chilly. Nick's chest hair was visible, as always, from underneath the collar of his golf shirt. The restaurant was busy – Tuesdays were buffet nights. Sofia hated buffets and insisted on ordering off the menu. In solidarity, I did the same.

Starters and main courses came and went. It wasn't until we'd asked the waiter for the bill that either of them brought up the subject of my gender. The conversation was polite and the two of them listened attentively as I expounded on issues of gender, sex and identity. I detailed how I'd realised the truth about myself, and explained my plan for my transition.

I looked for the gleam of understanding in their eyes that never came. They did their best to follow, though I could tell that none of it made much sense to either of them. Nick was determined that nothing would be different between the two of us, not even prepared to acknowledge that our entire dynamic would inevitably shift – he'd known me as someone I was not, and I wondered if he understood the gravity of the changes that I would undergo. Sofia was more open to acknowledging that she did not understand, but she would not let that rattle her. She clung to her live-and-let-live philosophy; as long as it didn't stop her from going to work, it was not something that she needed to be concerned with.

I knew these people had been my friends, but I also understood that concepts like being transgender or transitioning fell outside of any frame of reference they'd ever had. The entire subject was complex and confusing, even to me – but to them, it seemed simply not to matter at all, one way or the other. I didn't know whether to feel invalidated or relieved by their indifference.

I've learned to expect, and deal with, many kinds of reactions from people. Indifference, however, still threw me.

The viewing

Day –111, 12 March 2015

I had rushed home from work and quickly shaved, showered and dressed. Some light make-up, a casual T-shirt, jeans and some floral pumps, and I was ready to leave. I arrived at Rose's house about twenty minutes later, thoroughly excited for the evening's proceedings. It was a night I had been looking forward to for a long time, and I was so glad it had finally arrived.

* * *

Human beings are visual creatures by nature. The old adage is that a picture is worth a thousand words, although I suspect that to be a gross underestimation. When faced with something we struggle to understand, it's natural to want to see it with our own eyes – it makes the intangible tangible, brings the distant closer, and makes the strange more familiar.

I had met Toni through Rose – the two had been best friends for many years. Toni was a professional photographer who worked mostly with infants and families. I had an interest in photography, though I was decidedly amateur. Of course, I greatly admired Toni's work – her photos were always breathtaking, and she had a knack for capturing the human element in her subjects. So, when she'd said she wanted me to model for her, I had leapt at the opportunity. It was a wonderful chance to celebrate my new-found liberation from being camera-shy

The shoot itself had taken place in December. I could still remember Toni instructing me: 'Give a little smile!' 'Kick your booty out!' Four hours and seven outfits later, neither of us could believe how long we'd been at it. The shoot had been a wonderful experience for me. Until then, I'd only ever modelled for myself, with my self-timer or a remote control; although I'd managed some good shots, I was excited to see what a professional photographer would be able to do with me.

Our location, a flat that one of my friends was renting, was bright and uncluttered, with white walls and cream tiles and big windows that let the daylight in. I was comfortable around Toni, though this was the first time she'd seen me in person dressed as anything other than a boy. She was friendly and effervescent that day, as she always was, and immediately put me at ease. We sat together and picked the outfits we'd use, and I went to get changed into the first of them.

I had never modelled before, but Toni was superbly patient with me. She explained that the more uncomfortable the pose felt, the more natural it would look on camera. I twisted and contorted my body according to her expert instructions as she snapped away, forever reminding me to thrust my hips out further or to push my chin forwards and down when it inevitably started to drift away. She was great at positive reinforcement.

'Gorgeous!'

'You look beautiful!'

'Show off those killer legs!'

'Good girl, stunning!'

I *felt* gorgeous and beautiful and stunning. The experience was validating and empowering. At that point, I had not yet started on hormone therapy. Dysphoria still liked to play its tricks on me and chip away at my self-esteem. But that day, Toni was capturing me in my natural state, bringing out the beautiful and the feminine. There was no trace of the man I had once pretended to be.

She showed me a few photos off the back of her camera while we were shooting. Even seeing them on the small LCD display, I was floored. Later that afternoon, she'd quickly processed a photo to send to me as a sneak preview. It was gorgeous. A tear formed when I saw it. In the photo, I stood dressed in a black romper against the white wall. A pastel scarf that I held above my head flowed out behind me. I wore a smile that was wide, honest and genuine. I had not been used to smiling in photos before.

In the days and weeks that followed, that single photograph would act as my herald and emissary. It helped my therapist Meryl to visualise the real me. It convinced my psychiatrist Kevin that I was not in the least bit unsure of my identity. It allowed my friend Emily to understand that I was still the same person she'd known in university, but that I was becoming more authentic and happier.

It showed my mom that I had always been her daughter.

'Love it!' she said when she saw it. 'It's so you. I know that look!'

When I asked her what she meant, she told me she had a photo of me as a child with the same expression on my face – that smile that had been missing for so many years.

There must be apprehension and dread in the minds of friends or family about the appearance of their transgender loved one. Though they may be reluctant to admit it, I am sure their minds must, at times, turn towards the superficial – that they must begin to wonder, 'Isn't she just going to look like a man in a dress?'

That photo said very clearly, 'No, she most certainly is not.'

* * *

Rose hugged me warmly as I stepped out of the car. Inside the house, her mother and Toni waited, embracing me tightly in greeting as I entered. Coffee and chocolate and pastries were set out on the table in the middle of the living room. Toni was shaking with excitement – she was as eager to show me the photos as I had been to see them.

I kicked off my pumps and sat curled up on the couch, two of my closest friends at my side, as the slideshow started to play. Toni had selected a very fitting song to set it to:

We can go forever if we want to
We can live inside of a moment
The one that we own
You and me we got this
You and me we're beautiful, beautiful ...

I held back the tears as we watched. Each picture left me awe-struck. They all looked so natural – and shooting them had felt so natural. Toni's gaze was fixed on me, and her face lit up as I saw myself the way she had seen me through her lens. Occasionally, we'd all gasp simultaneously as an especially good shot appeared on the screen. Rose squeezed my hand as if to say, 'That's you up there,' but I was speechless.

Rose asked me if I'd feel comfortable having her mom see the photos. 'Of course,' I answered. I wanted the whole world to see them. To see *me*. She joined us on the couch, as we watched again and again.

'You look great in that photo!'

'What a wonderful picture of you!'

'Oh, you're so beautiful!'

For once, I did not struggle to believe the remarks.

It was a showcase of moments that I owned, moments in which I was beautiful. Moments that would not be the last.

One of the girls

Day –109, 14 March 2015

I sat at a table near the corner of the coffee shop as I waited for Elanah to arrive. The spot felt a little too trendy for me, to be honest – packed with youngsters sporting long beards or beanies, behind laptops at which they gazed through thick-rimmed spectacles. The decor was gaudy, far too ostentatious for my taste. It was unlike Elanah to be anything but punctual, though I realised that she may have been unfamiliar with the area. This was the second time that she and I were meeting in the space of a month – prior to that, I had not seen her in person for a good few years.

*　*　*

It had never occurred to me that it may have been unusual for most of my friends to be girls. It had just always been that way. Even as a young child of six or seven, the age at which children are supposed to become repulsed by the opposite sex (according to societal convention), I had always found it easier to make friends with girls.

In high school, when boys and girls attended classes on opposite sides of the school campus and seldom mixed, Elanah, my closest friend, had been a girl. She remained the only friend from those days with whom I had stayed in touch.

In the early days of university, I had kept to myself, mostly – I'd convinced myself that I was unskilled at socialising, given my cloistered adolescence, and didn't have the faintest notion of how to make friends. Nor did I have the desire to. But the nature of medical school is such that sooner or later, the class is divided into small groups, particularly for the practical components of the course.

This is exactly what happened when we began to study anatomy, and since I had made no friends – or even acquaintances – I had been randomly assigned to a group. Needless to say, the group consisted entirely of girls. This may not have been the statistical anomaly it seems, since two thirds of my class was female. Nonetheless, I failed to notice just how easy it was for me to fit into the group.

The rest of the group were already friends with each other, and before long they had 'adopted' me as one of their own. It didn't strike me as being peculiar at the time, but they had all been comfortable with me from the outset. I didn't understand, then, how significant it was that they did not feel threatened by my presence. They spoke candidly in front of me about boyfriends and bodily functions and fashion. They invited me along to the ballet. I accepted.

Even once we'd begun rotations and our small clique had become part of a larger group, one that included boys, I continued to feel more at home in the company of the girls. I must've been invited to boys' nights, but never went to any. I didn't have the faintest desire to go to the pubs or the strip joints or the paintball ranges. Bachelor parties I avoided with especial fervour, always having an excuse at the ready. I was, however, jealous of the kitchen teas to which I was never invited.

I had trouble understanding men, and difficulty identifying with how they thought. I'd often hear tales from my friends about heinous or callous behaviour that had been perpetrated by whichever man was currently the object of their affections, and would struggle to grasp how a human being could act towards another in such a way. Many of these men were self-centred and inconsiderate, which confused me. The patterns of behaviour that came naturally to them were foreign to me. It didn't make any sense that the label 'man' could apply to them and to me, when they felt like another species altogether.

Women, on the other hand, were far easier to understand. I could relate to them on an emotional level without having to try. I could speak more freely and feel more relaxed in their company than I ever could with men. I recognised that I was different from my peers and accepted this without giving it a second thought – I had figured out where I was comfortable, and where I was not. It all seemed like perfectly normal behaviour at the time.

I'd always been one of the girls.

*　　*　　*

Meeting Elanah had, at one stage, begun to feel like a bit of a chore. I was happy enough to let her talk and always willing to listen. But she had an intense personality, and when she started to get bored, she'd take to launching an onslaught of personal questions to keep herself entertained. I knew I'd have to muster the energy to keep my defences up and to hold her at enough of a distance to keep feeling safe. I hadn't realised why.

It had been about five weeks since I'd told her. She'd been a bit confused at first, but she'd done well to come to terms with it. I explained to her that I'd come to understand that gender had been the stumbling block for me for all those years, that it had put up walls between me and those I cared about. That I'd been shut off from her, as I had been from so many other people, and that I hadn't understood why until recently. That she was important to me, and that I wanted to rebuild our relationship.

Since then, seeing her had stopped feeling like a burden. I used to feel guilty for dreading our meetings; now, I looked forward to them. For the first time, I was able to let her in, in the way she deserved. She had always been a loyal friend to me, even when I'd kept her at such a distance. It was not without reason that she was the only one of my schoolmates with whom I still spoke.

A smile spread across my face as Elanah walked into the coffee shop. She'd managed to find the place, after all. She was heavily pregnant with her second child. Her silly grin was unmistakable, still one of her defining characteristics. She was as tall as I was, perhaps a bit taller even, with raven-black hair that was usually held up in a loose bun. I stood up to greet her, wrapping my arms around her and hugging her tightly. When I released her a few seconds later, she did not try to hide her surprise.

'I thought you didn't hug?'

'That was the old me,' I said.

My brother's sister

Day –102, 21 March 2015

It had been more than eight months since my brother had moved to Cape Town. We would talk every few weeks on the phone. He'd tell me how wonderful it was to live near the beach. How the air was fresher, the traffic quieter, how much better the coffee tasted. He'd ask about work, and I'd give him characteristically vague answers: 'Oh, the usual.' 'Ups and downs.' 'Busy, but okay.' 'Not too good, not too bad.'

I'd seen him twice since he'd left, when he'd travelled back up to Johannesburg for meetings or appointments. We'd try to make time to have a cup of coffee or a breakfast together. We'd speak about superficial things, and sometimes about things that were a little more personal. We'd discuss relationship problems and daddy issues and the weather. He'd ask me if I'd seen South Africa's most recent rugby game, or the latest blockbuster action movie. I'd shake my head, and we'd move on.

Even when we'd talk about our traumatic childhoods, the discussion would be far more academic than emotional. I had always looked up to my big brother. He'd been through many of the same kinds of experiences as I had, and he'd survived them with his dignity and self-respect intact. He had always been a man's man – a lover of fast cars, physical contests and shapely women. He owned a gun and several drills, read *FHM* religiously and had a mouth like a sailor. Fathering two daughters had softened him somewhat, but I still found it difficult to feel at ease around him. He'd always been a role model to me – not only that, but a constant and reliable source of support. It may not have been easy to connect with him in the way that I often felt he expected, but I knew that if I called, he'd come running.

I'd been on medication for about six weeks, and my body had started to change. I'd carefully chosen those to whom I'd disclosed, but so far I'd been met only with love, support and occasionally some mild shock or confusion. Of all the people in my life who were closest to me, Leo had been the last to know. Not because I didn't trust him or didn't care about our relationship. On the contrary, it was because – if anything – I cared too much. I wanted to tell him, and had wanted to tell him early. But I felt it would have been wrong to do it impersonally, and Cape Town was a long way away.

My work schedule was always busy. He and his family had just moved house, and were still settling in and unpacking and having renovations done. One of Cape Town's notorious wildfires was raging on his doorstep. I pored over the calendar, trying to find a day or weekend that I could steal to make the journey. I knew it would have to wait another month – there was just no way to reconcile the schedules and the stress that was even remotely practical. It tore me apart, but I knew it was for the best.

It was a Friday morning when I received a text from him. He'd be flying up for a meeting early on that Saturday, and departing again the following day. It would have been serendipitous, if that word weren't best reserved for situations that are jovial and light-hearted. As much as I wanted it to be, I knew that my imminent encounter with him would be anything but.

Leo was dark skinned, about my height, and very, very muscular. Ever since I could remember he'd been an avid gym-goer. He'd even coached me when I'd tried – unsuccessfully – to exercise my way out of the latent dysphoria I didn't know I had. He had a shock of black hair that was cropped short, though I remembered him letting it grow down to his shoulders when we were both younger. Salt-and-pepper stubble covered his face. He wore a tight T-shirt and a pair of cargo shorts. His trademark was a pair of brightly coloured sneakers; he owned several pairs. He'd chosen a brilliant orange pair on this occasion. He still had the mannerisms of a Joburger – his sentences were punctuated with 'howzits' and 'brus' and 'sweet, heys'.

He parked on the street outside my building and, since my flat was a mess, I came downstairs to meet him. We decided on a coffee shop – the local Europa – just a few blocks away. The skies had been cloudy earlier, but the sun beat down now in full force. It seemed a shame to drive the few hundred metres, so we walked along the main road. I hoped the clear skies were a portent.

The coffee shop itself was almost deserted at this time of the afternoon. We settled for a table in the corner, away from the street, the cars, the pedlars and the other patrons.

We exchanged small talk for a few minutes as I tried to keep myself distracted, hoping it would help me maintain the cool head and calm nerves that I was sure to need in just a few moments' time. By now, I'd come out face to face, on the phone and over the Internet. I'd tried leading into it with different lines, describing it in different terms. It never seemed to get any easier.

Then: 'I've been in therapy lately. Because I'm gender dysphoric.'

The words were starting to feel like a banner I could wave to make my loved ones feel less threatened while I set about dismantling or destroying or redefining a portion of their worlds. I knew nothing could really soften the blow of such a revelation. But in my mind, 'gender dysphoric' was still better than 'transsexual' or 'woman trapped in a man's body' or any of the other myriad expressions I could think of.

He didn't know what the term meant. Or, if he did, he didn't want to. He stared at me quizzically for a few moments, and I couldn't stop myself: 'Do you know what that means?'

'No.'

'I don't identify as male.'

'So, what does that mean?'

'It means I don't feel like I was ever supposed to be a man.'

'I still don't understand.'

I was silent for a few moments, my resolve already flagging.

'It means I'm a woman, I have always been and I'm going to live my life as one.'

I could see the confusion in his eyes. I'd known the revelation was going shake him, but I didn't know how he'd respond. I'd expected confusion, shock, maybe even sadness. What I had not been prepared for was hostility.

In the minutes that followed, I felt like I was on trial, trying desperately to plead my case to an unsympathetic jury. There's no rulebook for handling a loved one's coming out to you as transgender. But if there was, Leo would have broken every rule in it. I was subjected to an array of I-don't-see-its, how-do-you-knows and what-if-you-regret-its, interspersed with the occasional I-want-to-support-yous and a few I'm-just-worried-about-yous.

I was softly spoken and thoughtful in delivering my answers, but Leo kept interrupting me, the gravity of my disclosure clearly starting to weigh on him. His interjections were curt, and he spoke quickly as he hunched over the table as if to interrogate me. I knew he didn't mean to upset me, but it was difficult not to feel persecuted. Had it been a discussion with anyone else, I'm sure I would just have pushed back as hard as I was being pushed. But Leo was my big brother, to whom I'd looked up my entire life. I'd known that there were differences between us that I'd struggled to reconcile, but I had always respected him. And I couldn't bring myself even to think of fighting back.

He was relating to me from the position of a man, and I to him from that of a woman. In that moment, those differences between us became so much more apparent to me than ever before. I wanted to grab him, and shake him, and burst into tears and say, '*This* is what I mean!'

I told him that how to tell him had been weighing on me for a long time, how he'd been the only positive male role model I'd ever had, and how important it had been for me to do this face to face. He asked if I'd worried that he would reject me. I told him I knew he would accept me, and still love me. That I knew he wouldn't understand immediately, and had been scared he'd feel like he was losing his little brother. I couldn't have done a very good job of fighting back the tears, because he reached over and hugged me briefly.

I was exhausted, and Leo was still in obvious disbelief. By the time we'd settled the bill, the sunny skies had long since given way to dark clouds, and the rainfall was heavy and merciless. We sprinted along the pavement, ducking from canopy to canopy and trying to look for segments of road that were the least flooded when we needed to cross. Eventually, we were both standing in relative shelter outside my building. We said our goodbyes without an embrace, both thoroughly soaked.

I ran the remaining distance up the stairs and to my front door. Tears mingled with raindrops, and I could no longer see very clearly. I pulled off my wet clothes, wrapped myself in a towel, and buried myself beneath the blankets. The rain stopped sooner than the tears.

I was woken by the sound of my phone ringing, my brother's name on the screen. I took a few deep breaths before deciding that I was in no shape to talk, and swiped over the big red button. When he phoned back a second time, almost immediately, I realised that talking to him now couldn't possibly be worse than what I'd endured earlier that day.

'I just saw Mom. She showed me your photos,' he said. 'I think I understand now.'

I knew he was going to need time, but that he would eventually come around. I didn't expect it to happen so soon.

'I just want to support you, and be there for you, and for you to be happy,' he continued.

I held back more tears.

'I love you, no matter what,' he said.

'I love you too. Travel back safely and chat soon.'

A few hours later, my phone beeped with a text message.

I'm very proud of you. I can't even begin to understand what courage it must take to be as honest and true to yourself as you are. I love you and am here for you no matter what. Chat soon.

This time, the tears tasted less bitter.

Limbo

Day –100, 23 March 2015

The melancholy had a way of catching up with me at the strangest times. I lay in bed exhausted and frustrated, listening to the wind ravaging the trees outside the window of my second-storey apartment. I'd been through worse times before, and I was sure I would again, but on occasions like this, the quiet sorrow was pervasive and difficult to ignore.

The preceding week had been a good one. I'd been out a good few times, seeing movies, having dinners, visiting markets. I had been doing well with body image – I was attuned to the physical changes that were taking place, and found them pleasing and reassuring. I was making progress not only physically, but my relationships with friends and family had been improving too. I had felt full of love and warmth.

But sometimes, late at night, I'd be gripped by a pang of sorrow. Often, the trigger would be something trivial – a line in a book or an accidental glance at an old photo, or a fleeting memory of whispered words between lovers. Memories snowballed into memories, and emotions into emotions, in a self-perpetuating cycle.

The pain was not acute, but a dull ache that mounted into an overbearing sadness. I mourned my childhood scars, my adolescence spent in isolation, my lost young adulthood. I felt sorry for the child I had been, and I had sympathy for the adult I'd become.

I regretted the distance I'd kept from my loved ones. I tried to remember how it felt to be desired, and I wondered when – or even if – I would ever feel those sensations again. I ran my hands over my pale, hairless flesh, but nostalgia's caress was hollow. Tears formed but refused to flow.

Everything just seemed too in-between, too intangible. The sadness was too distant to cry about but too close to ignore, the losses corporeal enough to hurt, but too ethereal to confront. This was limbo, the grey area between sorrow and jubilation, exile and redemption, injury and convalescence. Male and female. The box in which *I* was the cat.

Lying in bed, I knew that time would pass, and that with it would come healing and hope. I waited for sleep finally to claim me.

Cosmic prank

Day –93, 30 March 2015

I sat in my carpeted office, at the old, scratched wooden desk that had been home to a string of doctors before me. The empty chairs on the opposite side of my desk were covered in upholstery that had once been bright, but had grown a little faded, as if they were tired of being sat on.

I'd never liked carpets – tiles always seemed so much neater. I couldn't help but wonder what lay beneath the well-worn carpet. It was a dusty brown, and scattered with odd stains. It continued to serve its purpose, but it had grown tattered and frayed in places.

The office had already been decorated when I'd first moved into it. A shelf against the back wall was lined with mismatched trinkets – glass vases, toy wooden boats and wire sculptures among them. They served to keep the shelves from looking bare, but I doubted that I'd have chosen them myself.

It had been a busy day at work – the stream of patients had been relentless, which had helped to distract me from my emotions. Having practical matters to attend to made it easier to sweep troublesome feelings under the rug. My solid work ethic and sense of duty had always meant I could put my own anguish aside.

My life had been in turmoil of late – doctors' appointments, therapy, coming out to friends and family. Everything seemed to be happening at once. My emotions were erratic, and at the best of times I'd feel like I was on the verge of a breakdown. I was sure that the oestrogen wasn't doing my mood any favours.

I toyed with a heart-shaped stress ball, left on my desk by some or other pharmaceutical rep, as I began to contemplate what would become of my career as my transition progressed. This was not the first time I'd thought about it. I was certain that I'd have to leave my current job – whereas we saw patients from a variety of races, cultures, religions and backgrounds, a good proportion of our business was Orthodox Jewish. The thought of having to explain concepts like gender dysphoria and transition to every patient who walked through the door was unbearable.

I had a vague notion of opening my own practice somewhere – a cosy little clinic, minimalist but comfortable, with a cleanly tiled floor and uncluttered shelves. It would be a place where patients could receive holistic health care, where they'd be treated like human beings instead of lab results or clinical diagnoses. Where everyone would be welcome without having to fear prejudice or judgement. Straight, queer, cis, trans – no one should have to face the kind of adversity that I had as a patient.

Being a doctor was not without its advantages. Even if the clinic of my dreams was not immediately practical, I imagined that I would be able to find a job *somewhere*. Of course, there would be a lot of bureaucracy to contend with – changing my name and identity documents, amending my university degree, updating my registration with the health professions council. Even acquiring letters of reference or recommendation from previous employers would be challenging, as they would have known me by a different name.

It was too early to deal with these matters. For now, I was secure in my job. But the prospect of having to tackle it all was daunting.

There were times when I struggled not to become overwhelmed by the magnitude of my 'predicament'. It was a downward spiral, as the traumas of the past weeks colluded to draw me deeper into despair. The stress of coming out to a multitude of people, several harrowing encounters with health-care professionals, uncertainty about my career and my future, and the frustration and anguish of dysphoria – each fed off and fuelled the others.

Aside from having a body that didn't fit correctly, I was not dissatisfied with the kind of person I had turned out to be. I often reminded myself that without the hardships I'd endured, I may not have been the same person.

But this was one of those days when it was difficult not to feel resentful. I felt like the victim of some cosmic prank. For nearly thirty years, I'd struggled to fit in. I'd put on an act for the whole world, and tried to convince myself that nothing was wrong with me. I was different from other men, and I'd known this for as long as I could remember. But I'd been too concerned about what I was not to have thought about what I was. Once I had, the pieces had violently crashed into place: a mind and a body so obviously incompatible with each other, and a journey to reconcile the two that would be arduous beyond measure.

A reality I hadn't chosen.

Why did it have to be me? Why had my wires become crossed? Why had I fallen victim to some bizarre hormonal glitch, before I had even been born?

How do you not be resentful when your very existence is difficult and your challenges feel insurmountable? When your odyssey is painful and confusing and unfair, how do you not bemoan the injustice of your circumstances and begrudge whichever coincidence or cosmic force or deity thrust it upon you?

Simply put, you don't.

But you try to treat yourself with the same compassion and understanding that you show to your patients. And then you stand back up and carry on, grateful that you are not without love and support. You remind yourself that you've already made it so far, and that you will make it further. That walking the path becomes less painful with each step, and that the burden will grow lighter with time. That one day, instead of sitting in this office with its rug that covers the feelings you've swept under it, you'll sit in the neatly tiled clinic of your dreams.

The Last *Seder*

Day –89, 3 April 2015

I reluctantly fastened my tie and rolled back my French cuffs, securing them with the pair of cufflinks that Dr Katz had given me the previous week. He had a passion for cufflinks, and he was something of a collector – the quirkier the better. This pair had little stethoscopes on them – he had his own pair that I'd often seen him wear.

This was the first invitation I'd accepted in a good few months. The invitations had become a bit sparser of late, but I knew that I'd felt much less comfortable with the idea of accepting them in any case, and I'd look for reasons to decline respectfully.

I knew that Dr Katz and his wife had noticed a change in my behaviour. Not at work, where my performance was about as good as it had ever been. But on the social front, I'd become much more of a recluse. The Jewish community is a small one, and word travels fast. So, Dr and Mrs Katz must have known that I had been in a long relationship, and that it had ended in August, almost eight months earlier. I hoped that would explain the change.

The truth is that Judaism is very concerned about matters of gender, and since I'd begun to come to terms with my gender identity, I'd felt increasingly uncomfortable in any sort of religious setting. Before I had been so plainly aware of what I was experiencing, it was simple enough to stand on the fringes, participating where it was appropriate, smiling politely and generally toeing the line. I may not have felt completely comfortable, but I was not being dishonest – I was doing my best to fit in with what I knew was expected of me. I may not have been raised entirely in accordance with the observances, but I knew well enough how to avoid making any embarrassing or disrespectful gaffes. Knowing that I identified as a woman made religious proceedings more challenging for me.

I had become accustomed to feeling a little lost on the rare occasions that I did go to the synagogue. But this time, I was entirely dissonant with my surroundings. It didn't help that I had arrived slightly late. I hurried past the stairway that led to the cordoned-off, upstairs women's section of the synagogue as I scurried into the main hall and found a seat next to Dr Katz. A silent nod was all the greeting we needed, as was often the case.

I opened the *siddur* (Jewish prayer book) with trembling hands, and willed my rapid breathing to slow. I'd been dreading this night since I'd had the invitation thrust on me a few weeks earlier. 'I won't take no for an answer,' Dr Katz had said; after trying out a handful of excuses on him, I realised he was serious. The most difficult part was already behind me – after a good, long chat about the matter with my therapist Meryl, I'd made the decision to not back out at the last minute with a case of debilitating, albeit fabricated, diarrhoea. I'd put on the uniform (a dark suit with a white shirt and a tie), I'd made it to the synagogue, and I'd found a seat. I'd even managed to get the prayer book open on the correct page. I was doing a perfectly good imitation of a nice Jewish boy – I just had to stay calm and remember that.

In a few hours, I thought as I continued to shake ever so slightly, *this will all be behind me.*

I glanced around the room, and I felt a brief pang of jealousy. The people around me were all content, standing in the synagogue in their dark suits and white shirts and boring ties. They knew their places and they knew their roles, and they were satisfied with them. Some of them had wives and children; of those who didn't, most – someday – would. They were secure in their identities. I reminded myself that my secrets were safe under my black-and-white penguin suit. I decided not to spend

112

any energy wondering which truths the rest of the congregation may have had hidden beneath theirs.

The service was over soon enough, unsurprising given my late arrival. I followed closely behind my host as he exited the synagogue, stopping to shake hands and exchange greetings with the rabbi, and then began the short walk to his home.

This was my third year in his employment, and though we'd spent the better part of each working day in offices mere feet from each other, the two of us had never shared a very close relationship. The practice was incredibly busy more often than not, and it was not unusual for days to pass with us exchanging nothing more than the odd hurried greeting. Certainly, we'd never spent any time on meaningful or personal discussions, although I had been a guest at Dr Katz's table on many occasions during those years.

His home was lavish but tasteful, and the man himself was simultaneously a great capitalist and a humanitarian. He worked long and hard hours, but I had always admired that he made time for his family. He knew when to be firm and when to be kind. In the time I had known him, I had grown to respect Jonathan quite deeply. Had I been shopping around for male role models, he would have been an excellent choice.

Seating arrangements were always a point of concern in the Katz household. The family was Orthodox, and the seats had to be arranged in such a way that men and women were not placed next to each other unless they were related. I briefly contemplated how a situation like mine may complicate the proceedings. I can't speak for other religions, but Judaism does not present a clear position on the subject of transgender issues: some authorities recognise and affirm transgender identities (although they fixate problematically on the point of surgery); many do not. Most of the religious texts themselves seem not to address the matter directly, if at all.

I was seated next to Brett, a gentleman just a couple of years younger than me who informed me that he was a towel salesperson. It's a fine line, trying to appear interested enough not to come across as aloof while not getting oneself dragged into conversation in excess of the bare socially accepted minimum. He was quite persistent, though he was amicable and good-natured. I made conversation as best I could.

And all the while I tried to keep from staring across the table at the women. Perhaps I would've felt less out of place seated among them.

The evening's proceedings were lengthy, as is to be expected at Passover. The ordeal is referred to as a *Seder*, which translates literally as 'Order' – everything has its place, and all the ritual and ceremony follows a precise structure. Generally, it lasts upwards of three hours; in an Orthodox household, it could easily exceed five. Much time is spent on relating and discussing the narrative of Passover, and the various symbols with which the *Seder* itself is concerned.

A fair amount of bloodshed and brutality forms the bulk of the Passover story. It was the sort of thing that I had tried before to justify or ignore, instead of acknowledging that these concepts made me uncomfortable with the religion into which I'd been born. But in recent months, I'd become more accepting of my own feelings, and I rationalised less and less. There were elements in the texts – specifically things like the wholesale murder of innocent people, the endorsement of slavery and violent vengeance – that I found disturbing, and that I could not reconcile with my own sense of justice, fairness and morality.

The *Seder* was a more intimidating prospect than it had been in years past, and the night itself came at the tail end of an emotionally harrowing week. I'd had some legitimate fears that I may simply burst into tears at the table. I felt like an outcast, seated amongst the men. Staying in character took effort and concentration, and I needed to be mindful not to let that show either. The suit and the tie and the cufflinks made an effective disguise, but one that I felt could prove insufficient under serious scrutiny.

I did my best to follow along with the proceedings, and I remained patient throughout the evening. I never wore a watch, and I imagine that not keeping track of time may have made it feel like it was passing a little quicker. Dinner was eventually served at close to ten o'clock and Mrs Katz's cooking was, as always, delicious. After dinner, the closing prayers were concluded within another hour, and I politely shook hands with my host and his guests as I took my leave.

I had attended many a *Seder* in previous years, ranging in severity from Reform to Orthodox. As I walked down the street, I realised how ironic it was that this had been the first *Seder* during which my own life had started to move towards any sort of order. I did not know if it was also to be my last, but I was certain that if there were to be any more in my future, I would spend them sitting with the women.

All the way

Day −83, 9 April 2015

'Unsettled' was not the word I'd have chosen to describe the state in which I'd spent the past day and a half. I'd been anxious and emotional, with the occasional bout of nausea. Uncertainty tended to have that effect on me.

I knew that it was not going to be possible to endure another day of being unsure. I always arrived at the practice earlier than Dr Katz, so I was lying in wait when he arrived. I calmly told him that I needed to finish the conversation we'd started two days before, and that the sooner it could happen, the better. He gave me a knowing nod, and reassured me we'd have a chance to conclude the discussion before the day's end.

* * *

It hadn't surprised me that there'd been a noticeable change in my behaviour over the past few months. I spent a great deal of time at work, and there were certainly days when it was harder to hide my depression or dysphoria or frustration. Some of the patients who knew me had remarked, on occasion, that I'd seemed a little subdued. They'd asked me if I was unwell; I'd dismissed their questions as nonchalantly as I could.

I was sure that the good days had slowly started to outnumber the bad. Although I still struggled with my mood and my body image, I spent much more time feeling good about myself, and hopeful for the future, than I had before. On a few occasions I'd let my guard down, even at work, allowing myself the freedom to be more open to my patients. For the most part, however, I still had a role to play – I had to be the brash, sarcastic, almost arrogant doctor that patients had come to expect.

Deception had been far easier for me when it had been subconscious, without the intent to mislead or subvert. It had started as a simple survival mechanism, an instinctive desire to minimise unwanted attention. As time passed, certain behaviours had become second nature. I'd known that there'd been *something* inauthentic in my interactions, but had spent less and less time fixating on it.

I had wondered how long it would take for Dr Katz to notice that something was off – or, if he had, when he would confront me about it. Two days earlier, it had happened. Jonathan had called me into his office and taken a seat next to me, on the patients' side of his desk. I had known that the discussion was going to be a serious one by the expression on his face. When he'd thrust a slab of chocolate at me, I'd realised that I'd been wrong – it was going to be a *very* serious one.

I'd tried to calm myself. The few minutes that were to follow were likely to be a turning point. Jonathan was an impressive specimen of a man. He stood well over six feet tall, and his voice resonated deeply even when he spoke softly. His hands were large and rough – it was clear that although he was an intellectual, he didn't shy away from physical labour. His large frame contrasted starkly with my delicate build.

He was always clad in a white shirt and a dark suit, the monotony of which he'd offset with colourful socks and quirky cufflinks. I'd noticed that he'd chosen a pair of penguins, and I'd focused on them as I'd tried to steady my breathing.

I had never been scared of Jonathan before, nor had I been as I'd waited for him to speak. Rather, I'd been scared of my secrets.

'You haven't been yourself lately,' he'd said, 'and I'm worried about you.'

I'd nodded sheepishly, but had stubbornly refused to break eye contact.

'I'm not a judgemental kind of guy,' he'd continued. 'I'm open-minded, and I leave my personal beliefs at home. I've noticed that there's been a change with you, and I'm concerned. Whatever it is, I just want to support you – there is nothing you can say that will distance me from you.'

'I came out of a seven-and-a-half-year relationship eight months ago,' I'd said, buying myself time as my thoughts had continued to race. 'It's not something you emerge from–'

'–unscathed,' he'd interjected.

I'd nodded. 'It took a toll on me. I'm still trying to recover.'

I'd swallowed hard, knowing that I'd stood at the crossroads. I could have left it there, or I could have trusted him. He had never given me reason not to.

'There's something else,' I'd said. 'I have gender dysphoria.'

I'd waited for the look of disbelief I'd become so proficient at identifying.

Only a few moments passed before he'd said, 'Okay. That's not a big deal.'

I'd been relieved, but had remained on edge. It's *always* a big deal – sometimes it just takes a bit of time for that reality to set in. He'd reassured me that he wanted to help me in any way that he could. He'd offered me time off, and enquired about my support structures. I'd assured him that I had friends and family behind me, and that I was seeing a team of professionals with experience in the field.

People's questions always helped me to gauge how well they'd understood the concept of gender dysphoria. They gave me a sense of where I stood and an opportunity to dispel any misconceptions.

None were forthcoming.

The promises of unconditional support had given me a degree of relief, but uncertainty had continued to plague me. I was 'out' to my employer and my colleague, but I wanted all the details to be on the table. I needed him to know that I wasn't sick and couldn't, consequently, be cured. That I had to transition, and that I'd begun to. That I'd uphold the commitment I'd made to see out the current year at the practice, and that I'd do so presenting as male. And that if, after that time, I had to leave, I'd do so without bitterness or resentment.

* * *

Jonathan and I sat down to conclude our conversation. This time we sat in my office, again on the patients' side of the desk. He paged absent-mindedly through a catalogue of shirts, ties and cufflinks as he waited for me to take my seat beside him.

'So, what exactly do you understand about this?' I asked, resisting the temptation to open with comfortable chit-chat.

'I know a bit about it, but I deliberately haven't read up since you told me,' he answered, 'because I don't want to be prejudiced at all. I want to support you through this as a friend, not as a professional.'

He began to tell me that he understood that there were two schools of thought about handling gender dysphoria.

'Some people think you should change the body,' he said, 'to bring it in line with the mind, though people are not always satisfied with the results.'

I cut him off.

'You're right,' I said. 'There's an incongruence between the body and the mind. And it's not possible to change the mind – all the studies show that any attempts to do so are unsuccessful, and it's regarded nowadays as being unethical.'

I realised that we'd each been trying to surmise the other's stance on the matter. The brevity of the short exchange belied its gravity. He nodded in understanding, and I knew that he'd taken the hint. He knew how I felt.

I went through the list of points that I'd mentally prepared. I told him that I had to transition, that I intended to see out my responsibilities at the practice, and that I did not want to jeopardise his business in any way. I told him that when the time came for me to start presenting as my true self, I was prepared to leave.

'Why?' he said.

I was stunned.

'You're one of the smartest and best doctors I've worked with,' he continued, 'and I don't see any reason why you shouldn't stay.'

Still stunned.

'I've never cared what anyone else thinks,' he said, 'and I'm not about to start. You may have to deal with adversity from patients, but as far as I'm concerned, you're welcome to work here for as long as you wish.'

He hadn't questioned me.

He hadn't fixated on my sexuality ('An idiot could see that it's not related to sexuality!' he'd said).

He'd acknowledged that he'd never be able to understand the conflict I'd endured.

I had always had a great deal of respect for Jonathan, a knowledgeable doctor, a supportive and loving father, a shrewd businessman and a respected philanthropist in his community. And still, he had shown me more compassion and had more insight than I would ever have expected.

He asked if he could have my permission to tell his wife, and I agreed without hesitation. Linda was an intuitive and gentle woman who'd always been kind to me. Based on what I'd heard through the grapevine it seemed that it was her concern, in the first place, that had led to the initial discussion. I thought it only fair for her know the truth, and Jonathan had reassured me that she, too, would be open-minded and discreet.

I told him that it was important for me to be honest with him, and that I had started on hormone treatment two months previously. We briefly discussed the changes that the hormones would bring about, and he didn't seem too concerned that anyone would notice. 'Our patients are too busy looking at themselves,' he'd said. He'd even gone so far as to reassure me that if

120

I wished, I could start presenting as female before the year was up. He was not concerned with formalities and technicalities, and only had my best interests at heart.

'Whatever you need to do, I am behind you *all* the way,' he told me, 'and I mean *all the way.*'

I thanked him sincerely, and told him how I appreciated his support and his understanding. Truthfully, I was still in disbelief. It was a conversation that I hadn't planned to have with Jonathan at that time. In fact, I wasn't sure whether it was a conversation I'd ever intended to have – no small part of me desired simply to part ways with him amicably. I'd have seen out the year, and then told him it was time for me to 'pursue my own endeavours', and spared him the confusion and the sympathy and the concern.

I did not doubt Jonathan's intentions for a moment. I wondered, though, whether as time passed the true weight of my identity would become clearer to him. Nonetheless, I breathed a sigh of relief.

I'd expected the worst, but allowed the tension to slip away.

Saying goodbye

Day 12, 13 July 2015

I park my car on the side of the street, around the back of the practice. In the two and a half years that I had spent working there, I had always parked inside, in the small parking lot with its prominent Doctors' and Staff Parking Only signage. There is something comforting about parking around the corner. It gives me a modicum of privacy while I steel my nerves, and it gives me the safety of knowing that I can still flee unseen.

Despite that, I know that it is too late to turn back. My departure two weeks before was abrupt. I need closure, and all the unsaid goodbyes need to be spoken. Besides, I have already armed myself with cakes from the nearest kosher bakery. I am determined not to let them go to waste.

The week before, I'd made it as far as the entrance to the bakery before turning back. The trepidation and apprehension had been overwhelming. The idea of marching back into the practice with head held high had been an appealing one, but the reality of it was frightening. I'd found myself fixating over the minutiae – even just the prospect of walking up to the door and ringing the bell had been terrifying.

I allowed myself to back out then, but it had weighed on me since. The sooner I face this, the sooner I can stop worrying about it. I remind myself that I have nothing to fear. There is no need to hide any longer.

My heart races, and small beads of sweat form on my forehead. I take a few deep breaths.

Stace, I say to myself, *you're doing so well. You've got this.*

A few more breaths, and I pick up the cakes.

* * *

Leaving the practice was something that I had been expecting for a long time, but the reality of it had still come as a shock. My dysphoria at having to present as male day in and day out at work had become increasingly intense. It had worsened since I had transitioned socially, refusing to present as anything other than female in any other setting. I sat drearily at my desk most days, feeling like a prisoner. Getting dressed for the office in the mornings was something I had come to dread. Some days I almost failed to make it out of the house, held back by my own tears as I stood in front of the mirror.

Jonathan's initial response to my revelation had been to say that my gender identity didn't make a difference. But it did make a difference, in truth. To everything. As time had passed, the magnitude of my admission had begun to settle on him, and he had started to realise the impact it could have on his practice.

He went to great pains to assure me that he cared for me deeply, that he respected me as a doctor and as his fellow human being. He told me how desperately he had wanted to stand by me on my journey, and how intensely he regretted that he could not. He worried that his patients, a large number of whom were Orthodox Jews, would struggle to accept me. He relied on his business to support his family. It was a risk he could not afford to take.

I never doubted his sincerity. Jonathan had been one of the few men in my life whose integrity I respected. This had been the outcome I'd expected when I'd first come out to him.

He'd often approached me with suggestions about where I may find work. He had contacts in emergency rooms and academic departments with whom he promised to put me in touch. His concern for me was genuine, and he was trying to do every bit he could to make my journey easier.

We hadn't settled on a date for my departure. I had already told him a few weeks earlier that outside of the workplace, the person he knew me as had ceased to exist. My new life had taken hold of me. I was sure that the anguish I experienced at work playing the role of the manly doctor was, by then, very apparent.

A few days before the end of the month, I learnt that patients had begun talking about me. Someone had caught sight of an Anastacia Tomson on Facebook, and despite my profile having no links to my deadname, I had been recognised. Word had started to spread in this small Jewish community. I was surprised it had taken so long.

It wasn't long before Jonathan asked me if I knew that people had started to talk. I told him that I did, and that it didn't especially bother me. I had panicked briefly when I first heard that the news was spreading, but I'd quickly calmed myself down. As the news became increasingly public, the matter of my still coming to work became more urgent. It was two days before month-end when Jonathan came to talk to me.

'What kind of time frame do you have in mind?' he asked. A polite way of saying, 'When do you plan to leave?'

'I don't know,' I answered, 'but sooner is better.'

'End of the month?'

'Sure.'

And that was that.

Two days later, I had all the belongings in my office packed into two small carrier bags: my stethoscope, my pens, my notebooks and a few trinkets I'd accumulated from the pharmaceutical reps over the past two years. I scooped up the branded thermometers, plastic tape measures and colourful flexible rulers, deciding what to throw away and what to take with me. I glanced at the walls from which, just a few weeks earlier, I'd taken down all the paintings that had hung there since before my arrival and replaced them with my own photographs. I decided to leave the photographs up, as a legacy of sorts.

Leaving the practice was always going to be bittersweet. In my time working there, I had not just seen patients and treated illnesses. I had interacted with people and built connections. I had been so much more than a doctor. I had been a friend, a counsellor, a confidant.

But I had also been a prisoner of society's rigid expectations.

It was well after 6 p.m. when Jonathan finished seeing his last patient. Most of the practice staff had already left. He came into my office.

'How are you feeling?' he asked.

I choked on my words. 'I don't know,' I answered. 'It's bitter-sweet. I know I have to move on, but this is hitting me harder than I expected. What about you?'

'It's a lot to process. I wish there could've been another way.'

'Thank you,' I stammered. 'It's been an honour and a privilege to work here with you.'

'The privilege was all mine,' he replied.

'I'm sad to be leaving, of course ... but I do it without regret. I have to leave this life behind that doesn't fit.'

He emphasised again how he respected me, as a professional and as an individual. He told me he was saddened that he could travel no further with me along my path.

Before, he would have shaken my hand, or reached to hug me. But that evening, he did not. It was not an affront, but an affirmation: Jewish law forbade him from social physical contact with a woman to whom he was not married or directly related.

*   *   *

I stand at the door of the practice, and gingerly ring the bell. There is a buzz at the gate as the electromagnetic latch releases, and I pull it open. I walk up to the reception desk, cakes in hand. Behind it sits Jonathan's mother, who often worked as a receptionist, and Judy, the practice nurse.

'Good afternoon, ma'am,' his mother says. 'How can I help you?'
She doesn't recognise me. Of course she doesn't.

Jonathan was the only one at the practice whom I'd told, but in the past few weeks the news that I was transitioning had spread like wildfire. I had no doubt that the rest of the staff at the practice had already heard.

'No, I don't think you can,' I answer. 'But maybe I can help you.'
She stares at me quizzically.

Good, I think, realising that even my voice hasn't given me away. *Speech therapy must be working.*

'I brought cake,' I go on, 'to make up for not having had the chance to say goodbye properly.'

They recognise who I am.

'You look wonderful,' Judy exclaims. 'And so happy!'

Jonathan's mother tries to busy herself with a pile of papers on the desk.

'Yes,' I reply, 'I'm better now. I'm doing what I have to do.'

We exchange pleasantries for a few minutes, until Jonathan emerges from his office. He eyes me for a moment or two before he bursts into a wide smile.

I spend a few more minutes chatting with everyone before I take my leave. As I walk towards the car, I breathe a sigh of relief. I did myself proud. I walked in, bravely and honestly. I said my goodbyes, the truth of who I was displayed boldly and without shame.

Well done, Stace, I whisper to myself as I open the car door. *You've got this.*

Thank you for noticing

Day –67, 25 April 2015

I looked at my watch – 7:30 p.m. I reminded myself that I should have told Zach that the reservation was half an hour earlier. He inevitably ran late, and I inevitably forgot. I reassured myself that he and his fiancée Nadia would arrive soon, and that the restaurant would not throw a fit if we were ten or fifteen minutes late. I realised I was panicking over minutiae, but I'd been on edge the whole day.

* * *

I had met Zach four years earlier. He was tall and skinny, with a perpetual blonde goatee and a shaggy mop of hair. He usually wore baggy jeans and a dark T-shirt with a print of skulls or monsters or a lightning storm or wolves on it. I had been living in Nelspruit, a good three hundred kilometres away from home, working in a state-run hospital as all newly qualified doctors are required to do. I'd realised, when applying for a post, that there was a better-than-even chance that I'd be sent off to some small, distant, rural town, so I'd decided to ask for one in a scenic part of the country, at least.

Nelspruit itself had not been unpleasant – it had grown tremendously from the one-horse town it had been in my childhood to something of a metropolis, with all of the amenities of a bigger city. Its inhabitants were still largely quite conservative, though. Since Jennifer and I had always been rather liberal, it took some time before we made any friends there.

Eventually, we had met a group of people with whom we'd got along quite well, but we'd had to leave most of them behind when we'd moved back to Johannesburg. Zach had moved to Johannesburg himself, so we'd remained in touch. My relationship with him had grown more distant than it had been in Nelspruit. We didn't talk as often, and months often passed without us seeing each other.

It had been two months since I'd come out to Zach. He'd been surprised and had insisted that he was accepting, though I was certain that the gravity would take some time to become fully apparent to him. We'd seen each other more frequently, and each time I'd talk a little more about the process I was going through, trying to help him to understand that as time passed, my body and my presentation would change.

Zach had always viewed me as a role model of sorts. I had always been very uncomfortable with feeling that I had to set an example for someone else when I was so far from being at peace with who I was myself, but disclosing to him had freed me of much of that burden. It meant, of course, that our dynamic was going to change – it had to. Perhaps we'd never be as close as he used to want us to be. But wherever it left our friendship, at least it would be in a place that was honest instead of manufactured.

I'd told him that he should tell his fiancée. She and I had only met once, but we'd got along well. It was clear to me that she was socially progressive, and I was sure she wouldn't have much difficulty understanding. Since they planned to marry in the coming months, I thought it important for the two of them to understand that there was a good chance I'd be presenting exclusively as female by their wedding. Who knew – perhaps I'd even be a bridesmaid?

Two days earlier, I had gone with Zach and Nadia to watch a roller derby match at a nearby sports venue. Nadia was quite enthusiastic about the sport, and was always keen to share its intricacies with newcomers. I'd met the two of them outside the arena – it was the first time either of them had seen me presenting as female.

I had been so curious to see how Zach's attitude to me was going to change. By that time, I had already made it quite clear to him that I was in the process of transitioning. He'd seen photos, and I'd spent a fair amount of time talking to him about the process and the changes that I was expecting to happen. And I'd been able to see his level of understanding increase each time we'd met. But I was certain that seeing me in person for the first time would change things between us. He already knew the facts on an intellectual level, but I was sure that witnessing the change for himself would give him an emotional understanding of who I really was.

When they'd arrived, Nadia had greeted me warmly, shouting 'Hey, gorgeous!' as she'd rushed to embrace me. Zach had been still for just a moment as he'd watched. He'd contemplated for a moment, then had reached out to hug me. I'd risen onto the tips of my toes – Zach was a good half a foot taller than me – as he'd drawn me into his arms, a silent affirmation that the handshakes we had always shared before were now a thing of the past.

The evening had been pleasant and comfortable. I had felt natural, liberated and peaceful. Everything had fallen into place, just as I'd known it would.

* * *

At 7:35 p.m., the bell finally rang. *Only twenty minutes late,* I thought. *Better than I expected.* I had been for my fourth session of laser just a few hours earlier. The skin on my face did not react badly to the treatments, but had been left sensitive enough that any idea of shaving or applying make-up was entirely out of the question until at least a day or two had passed. It meant that I was forced to spend the day and the evening presenting as male.

Zach and Nadia greeted me as I walked down to meet them. Zach began to stretch out his hand towards me and caught himself halfway, pulling it back and wrapping his arms around me instead. I breathed a sigh of relief, and we began the short walk to the restaurant, just a few blocks away.

The restaurant was a recently opened spot in a strip of trendy Norwood eateries. They played no music there, but the buzz of conversation from within was audible even before we'd reached the door. The walls were decorated with an assortment of black-and-white photographs, old-style poster advertisements for Coca-Cola, and a variety of framed maps. Two large wood-fired ovens stood opposite the entrance. As I entered, the heat from the ovens was palpable. It contrasted starkly with the cool evening breeze out on the street.

'Table for three, sir?' the waiter asked me.

Sir.

The word was as jarring as always.

I'd made the reservation under my deadname, aware at the time that the laser session would force me to present as male for the evening. In the months that had passed, I'd taken to using my initials rather than my name whenever I could. I'd become skilled at avoiding the use of gendered pronouns or epithets when talking about myself to others. I reluctantly gave my name to the waiter. The name was as ill fitting as my appearance, and I reassured myself that it would not be long before I could leave both of them behind.

It was already apparent to me that, having met the 'real' me, both Zach and Nadia's attitude towards me had changed. They had seen me for who I was, and understood that my identity didn't change based on what I was wearing. Even dressed as a man, I felt more comfortable in their company than I had before, just knowing that they'd had that glimpse of my truth a few nights earlier.

Nonetheless, one's presentation always has a subconscious influence on one's behaviour and demeanour. I may have been more comfortable, but I was still on edge. Zach proved it to me when, somewhere between the starters and the main course, he turned to me and said, 'You really don't like being in boy mode, do you?'

'No, I do not,' I replied. 'But thank you for noticing.'

Everything?

Day –46, 16 May 2015

I spent the morning at the Department of Home Affairs, the sacred government institution responsible for keeping records of the personal details of every South African citizen, the faceless, heartless entity responsible for issuing and validating identity documents, birth certificates and passports.

Of course, neither my sense of self nor my identity was contingent on a piece of paper. By that time, I was more than certain about who I was. But my own certainty was not enough to convince the bank, or the university that had issued my degree, or the professional body whose sanction I needed to practise as a doctor. It was not enough to convince customs, or passport control, or the traffic department. My ID book, my driver's licence, my credit cards – each betrayed me, reminded me of a fictitious persona that never should have existed.

Bureaucracy is a fickle beast, almost universally abhorred yet universally required. Paperwork and documentation and official stamps – all absurdly hard to come by, but necessary for successfully navigating the world.

I had known for a while that sooner or later I would have to face the beast head on. To venture, bravely, deep into the cold stone walls of Home Affairs, to lay down, in order, all the forms and papers that detailed who I had been and who I was meant to be, to plead my case in front of this behemoth, and to petition The System to acknowledge my true self.

Of course, I did not arrive unprepared. I had spent the past few weeks scrutinising the requirements for this procedure and collecting the requisite paperwork. An original birth certificate, signed affidavits from my mother and me, letters from doctors that confirmed I had undergone medical gender reassignment. And of course, certified copies of them all, just in case.

I'd asked those who had been through this process before for advice to learn about their experiences, find out which barriers they'd had to overcome, and determine exactly how they'd managed to sweet-talk the clerks to get what they had come for.

My situation was complex – I had a number of erroneous details that needed amendment. Of course, my gender, as recorded in the national birth registry, needed to be corrected. It goes without saying that I needed to change my forename. The one I had been given was highly gendered – there'd never been any desire on my part to retain it. And, to complicate matters further, I had decided to change my surname. I'd elected to abandon my abusive father's name in favour of my mother's maiden name.

It had been many years since he'd disowned me.

I'd been told that it was possible to have these three changes processed simultaneously, though I was warned that the clerks may need a little coercion. Gender amendments were still relatively rare in South Africa. They were difficult and time-consuming, so much so that Home Affairs staff would look for any excuse to turn applicants away.

The queue was long, and the building was overcrowded, poorly maintained and uncomfortably stuffy. I was given a stack of forms to fill out when I entered, and I completed them meticulously, taking care to ensure that my handwriting was impeccable. The last thing I wanted was a misspelled name when this ordeal finally came to an end. I made it to the front of the queue and was eventually called up to the counter.

The clerk was a woman in her fifties, her dyed red hair contrasting starkly with her grey cardigan. She wore a name badge that proclaimed her as Magda. She peered up at me from behind the thin, severe rims of her spectacles.

A moment or two of awkward silence passed, and I realised

that the cold stare was as much of an acknowledgement or greeting as I was likely to get.

'Hello,' I said. 'How are you?'

Her silence was palpable as she continued to stare at me, fingertips rapping the desk impatiently.

'I need to apply to have some changes made to my ID,' I stammered.

'What sort of changes?'

'Name, surname and gender. Please.'

She ripped the stack of documents from my hands and shuffled through them, mumbling to herself.

'You know this is a complicated process, don't you?' she eventually replied.

'Yes, I do,' I responded, 'and I'm so sorry to have to worry you with it, but I really appreciate your help.' *Catch flies with honey*, I thought.

She stared up from the papers and regarded me for the first time since I'd approached the counter. I watched as her gaze slowly shifted across me, top to toe and back again.

She thought silently for a moment, her eyes still fixed on my face.

'*Ag*, but you're a cute little thing, aren't you?' she offered, as her stony expression broke into a smile.

I shifted uncomfortably, knowing that the worst was probably still to come.

'Let me just go check with my supervisor that these papers are all in order,' she said, the effort of leaving her seat clearly weighing heavily upon her.

She scuttled off through a dilapidated door into the dark recesses of the building. It must have been a good ten minutes before she returned.

'My supervisor will come to take a look as soon as she can. But I just need to check with you,' her gaze narrowed, 'have you had *everything* done?'

I had prepared for this moment, but it still came as a shock.

Everyone I'd asked had warned me that this was going to happen. In South Africa, the law, as it relates to amending one's gender marker on the population registry, is quite clear: the applicant needs to have undergone medical gender reassignment, and proof of this needs to be submitted to the Department of Home Affairs by way of two confirmation letters from medical professionals.

The legislation doesn't care about the specifics of the reassignment itself. Surgery is not a prerequisite of any kind. *Any* form of medical intervention fulfils the criteria. As long as the supporting letters corroborate that reassignment has taken place, no further information or investigation is necessary. Private parts are not the concern of anyone except the individual to whom they belong. In the lay person's terms: the Department has no right to ask what is between anyone's legs.

Unfortunately, the Department seems not to know this.

(One of the tragic realities facing transgender people is that others seem to think that they have the right to intimate details about our bodies. Imagine, for a moment, that you're shopping at a grocery store. You've filled up your trolley, and you're waiting at the checkout line. At last, it's your turn. You approach the cashier, and start to load your groceries out onto the counter.

'How are you?' she asks.

'Fine thank you,' you reply.

'Do you have a loyalty card?'

'No, sorry.'

'Do you need bags?'

'Yes, please.'

'What's between your legs?'

'Excuse me?'

'Your genitals,' she says. 'What do you have?'

You stare blankly at her.

'What is between your legs?' She is insistent, despite your obvious discomfort. 'A penis? A vagina? Something in between?

Well, what is it?')

'Have you had *everything* done?' the clerk asked again, as if it were the most innocuous question in the world.

'Yes,' I replied.

'Everything?' she pressed. 'Even the surgery?'

Every muscle in my body begin to tense up. All I wanted was to be able to pull out an identity document that matched who I was. To have a driver's licence that had my own name and photograph on it instead of someone else's. Not to have to answer awkward questions every time I need to identify myself to explain why my paperwork bore what was traditionally a man's name. The freedom from anxiety that is every cis person's birthright, and every trans person's dream.

The activist in me was sorely tempted to cause a scene right there in the middle of Home Affairs. But that wouldn't help me to go to job interviews. It wouldn't help me in a police roadblock. It wouldn't help me to get through passport control.

'From a medical point of view, I am entirely female,' I stated as matter-of-factly as I could.

It wasn't a blatant lie, though in this situation, even that would have been acceptable. I'd been for blood tests a few weeks before, and my hormonal balance was that of a cisgender woman.

'Okay, good,' she replied. 'Because we need everything to have been done in order to process this.'

Her supervisor, at last, emerged from the door in the back of the room, her fingertips glistening with grease.

She approached the desk, and grabbed the stack of papers, scrutinising each one intently. She flipped through them slowly, until she came to the doctors' letters. She put them down on the desk and read through each one, tracing each word with her finger as she did so. Every so often she looked up at me, before returning her attention to the documents in front of her.

Eventually, after much mumbling to herself, she lifted her nose from the papers.

'It all seems in order,' she sighed, reluctantly admitting defeat.

The clerk grabbed the stack of forms, and began filling out the requisite sections, applying her rubber stamp where it was required, sorting and stapling and signing and shuffling her way through them.

Before long the paperwork was completed – signed, stamped and fingerprinted in what I hoped were all the right places. The sticky ink still clung to my fingers, despite my best efforts to rub it off with the few scraps of paper towel I could find at the neglected fingerprint station.

The clerk told me that the process could take anything from six to nine months. Six to nine months without an accurate form of identification. I consoled myself: however long it may take, it had begun.

'It's unfair though,' she remarked as she led me to the door. 'Look how gorgeous you are!'

That's not what's unfair, I thought bitterly.

I bit my tongue and thanked her for the compliment.

Potpourri, Part 2

Day 14, 15 July 2015

As I pull up to Dianne's driveway, the gate opens for me. I spy Dianne's smiling face through the window as I drive in and park. She greets me with a hug and leads me inside. Michaela is already seated, her lap playing host to Dianne's black-and-white cat.

'Staci!' she exclaims as she leaps up to hug me.

Michaela is clearly happy to see me again after all these months. The cat, on the other hand, seems somewhat less impressed by my arrival.

* * *

It had been a few months since I had last attended the gender support group, with its colourful assortment of members. There had been multiple reasons for my protracted absence, all of which were perfectly reasonable, but I had still felt a pang of guilt as each Wednesday evening had passed.

When I had first joined the weekly meetings, the group had been a safe space, one that allowed me to grow and explore and learn. I had been frightened, neither knowing what to expect nor fully understanding the new language to which I suddenly found myself exposed.

As time progressed, I grew more comfortable with the meetings. I became less afraid to share my experiences. It was in those meetings that I was first called by my chosen name, and where I experienced the euphoria that stems from being referred to with the correct set of pronouns.

One of the issues I did grapple with at the meetings in those early days was survivor guilt. Many of the group's members were young. They were students, financially dependent on others – usually their parents – for support. Some of them had been abandoned by their families, and struggled to make ends meet. A few had track records of admission to psychiatric units. Many of them had horror stories about the experiences they'd endured at the hands of transphobic medical professionals. Some of them had received threats of physical violence in public.

And then there was me – a doctor with a stable job, living on my own. I had never encountered the discrimination or harassment that seemed to be such a prominent feature in so many of the others' day-to-day lives. I felt like I hadn't paid my dues.

It had been worse when I was still questioning my own identity, gingerly treading the space between binary and non-binary at a time when the prospect of transition seemed unattainable. A time when I could foresee no way in which I could reconcile the rest of my life – my career, my family, my desires and goals and expectations – with the notion of transition. I made every excuse I could conceive of. I told myself that I was too old, too weak, too uncertain. That even if I did transition, it would not make me comfortable in my own skin. I tried so desperately to make myself believe that some part of me *did* identify as male, that I could live a life that straddled the genders.

I told myself that I may be trans but I was not trans *enough*.

Doubt and fear are some of dysphoria's most powerful agents. Paralysed by dread and uncertainty, I sought out every reason to judge myself and to find myself unworthy.

Over time, as I continued to go to the group's meetings, I came to understand that identities are not defined by the hardships they often attract. I was reassured to hear from other members that they, too, had experienced similar insecurities. Their diverse narratives bolstered me. Those who I regarded as wiser than me encouraged me by acknowledging that gender is, in fact, a big, scary, intimidating thing. I started to feel like it was acceptable to be scared, and that I didn't have to punish myself for it.

The uneasy life I had led before, the one that had insidiously become my normal, now stood in stark contrast to the life that lay before me. The insecurities that had slowly accumulated over the years, which I had trained myself to ignore, were plainly visible, and their extent was shocking. I knew there could be no more excuses. Work, family and life would have to fit into the journey I knew I had to take.

Over the past few months, life had become chaotic. Wednesday afternoons were the only time off I had during the week, and soon they were filled with medical appointments. I found that I no longer had the time to attend the group's meetings regularly. Once I had started to make my peace with who I was and what I had to do, I began to pursue my new life aggressively. I no longer needed the reassurance that the group had once given me. At the same time, I wondered if there was much that I could contribute to others. I felt like I'd entered a new stage of my development, that I was changing and learning and growing into myself. It was a time when I needed to focus on myself.

*   *   *

As I sit down beside Michaela, other people begin to arrive. There are new members, whose faces I do not recognise, and old ones whom I've missed. I am overwhelmed by the sudden realisation of the extent to which my life has changed in the intervening time.

Six months of hormone therapy have changed the shape of my body, while speech therapy has altered my voice. It has been weeks since I left my job. I have applied for legal changes to my name and gender on the national population registry.

I am not the only one. Sam, who had given me so much guidance in my fledgling days, has just started their own non-binary transition, and is celebrating their third week of testosterone treatment. Taylor no longer identifies as genderqueer – she is a woman, and she has chosen the name Rachel. Dianne's hair has grown long enough to tie up, and she has been to apply for her gender amendment at Home Affairs.

I sit back in my seat, comfortable and relaxed. Gone is the survivor guilt and any notion that I harboured, once, of not being trans enough.

I have something to give back. And I am glad, at last, to do just that.

Breaking the silence

Day 20, 21 July 2015

The waitress leads me to a table in the middle of the noisy coffee shop. I sit as she places a menu in front of me.

'What can I get you to drink, ma'am?' she asks.

I look up at her, making eye contact and pausing for a moment.

'I'll have a green tea, thanks,' I say, loudly enough to ensure I am heard over the ambient noise.

To anyone watching, it looks like a fairly straightforward exchange. And on this occasion, it is. A few months before, it would not have been.

*   *   *

I first met Michelle Reid on a Tuesday afternoon, almost four months earlier. She'd been recommended to me by my psychiatrist when I'd asked him if he knew of any speech therapists who would be sympathetic to my plight. He'd given me a list of three names and contact numbers. Michelle's name had been the first on the list, and she also happened to be the closest.

I was cautious when I approached her. I sent her an e-mail from my professional account, the one that started with Dr, simply asking if she did work with transgender patients, specifically trans women. She replied within a few minutes, telling me that although she'd only briefly treated one such patient before, she was willing to try to assist.

I explained the intricacies of the situation – that the patient's job still required her to present as male, but that she hoped to leave it soon. And that she was tremendously dysphoric about her voice, and was desperate to start working on it.

Michelle got back to me quickly again, confident that she'd be able to help. I breathed a sigh of relief. The technicalities were all behind me, the complexities of the situation were out in the open, and she'd insisted they weren't a problem. All that remained was to tell her that the patient was me.

My first appointment was scheduled during one of my lunch breaks. I rushed off to her rooms, worried that I'd be late. I arrived, as it happened, in good time – traffic had been light. I paced the corridor of the medical centre until I reached the office that bore her name on its frosted glass window. I rang the bell, and the receptionist let me in.

Classical music filled the waiting area as I filled in the form that the receptionist handed to me, grudgingly completing the fields that demanded my deadname and the sex I'd been assigned at birth. I sat on the dark brown couch in the corner as I waited.

A tall woman dressed in dark jeans, white-soled sneakers and a red long-sleeved top emerged. Her long, dark hair was clipped back and hung straight down her back. She smiled at me broadly as she greeted me, and I responded with a sheepish grin.

She led me through to her office, and I sat down, arms crossed tightly in front of me. She was friendly and her demeanour was warm, but I found it hard to feel comfortable sitting in front of her dressed in a shirt and tie, trying for the sake of my job to look as much like the manly doctor I was supposed to be as I possibly could.

I had already been working through some voice exercises I'd found on the Internet and when she set up her iPad to measure my pitch, Michelle was amazed at the frequencies I was able to reach. She reassured me that I'd been doing well, and that it all looked very promising. At one point in the session, she even went as far as to say, 'You already have the voice! You just need to learn how to use it.'

When I first started seeing her, I'd been on hormones for just over two months. But hormones, if you are a trans woman, do nothing to help your voice. A surge of testosterone during puberty thickens the muscles of the vocal cords, irreversibly altering the range of frequencies that they produce. Hormones don't undo those changes. The only ways to compensate are with risky surgery that leaves a good deal of patients hoarse or with hours of hard work, preferably with a speech therapist.

In addition to measuring my voice, Michelle expressed an interest in the rest of my experiences. She wanted to understand me. I recognised her genuine concern, and it helped to put me at ease.

I tried to explain exactly why I'd come to see her. My voice was holding me back. Even in the early days of my hormone therapy, my appearance seldom betrayed me – until I had to speak. I was afraid to open my mouth. My voice had never been especially deep or gruff, but it was never mistaken for feminine. It crippled me. The problem wasn't that it gave me away as being transgender, because that was not something of which I was ashamed. It was that even when I was presenting in a manner that was completely and unmistakably feminine, my voice meant I'd be misgendered. The visual evidence was convincing, but once salespeople, shop attendants and wait staff heard me speak, they'd immediately revert to calling me sir: a knife through the heart.

My voice was not a matter of vanity, it was a matter of confidence – my security in my identity and in my ability to have that identity acknowledged by those around me. So, for the months and weeks that had passed, I'd resigned myself to silence. I limited myself to settings in which I'd have sympathetic friends with me who'd speak on my behalf.

When I finished relating my story, Michelle was visibly moved. I had no doubt that she understood just how important a role she was to play in my journey.

I had weekly appointments with her, working first on sounds

and then progressing to full words and sentences and speech. I spent hours at home practising, recording my voice and listening to it over and over again. I gradually dismantled the mental block against speaking that I'd established as a means of self-defence.

'I'm done seeing you like this,' she said one afternoon as I was walking out of her office.

I didn't understand. We'd been making such good progress ... everything had been going well.

I regained my composure. 'What do you mean?'

'Like this. Dressed like this, acting like this. It isn't you. I need to work with the real you now.'

'Oh.' My cheeks grew warm as I spoke. 'I understand. I've been thinking the same thing, actually.'

We arranged from then on to schedule my appointments with her at times when I'd be able to present as female.

The first opportunity I had was six weeks after my first encounter with her. Michelle had already seen photos, but she was taken aback to see me in person. She told me how much prettier I was in real life, and remarked on how different my behaviour was. I was much more relaxed. I was myself; gone were the stiff posture and the rigid hands and the hunched shoulders.

As the weeks continued to pass, I astonished myself with the progress I made. Michelle watched as I grew and flourished. As I worked with her on perfecting my voice, I abandoned the male guise in all settings outside of work.

Although she'd been relatively inexperienced in treating transgender patients when I'd first started seeing her, she put a tremendous amount of effort into research – she watched countless voice-training videos produced by trans women, and she read all the literature she'd been able to find on treating transgender voices. We learnt and grew together as I sat in her office week after week, practising scales and chants, trying to tighten my larynx, learning to speak from my throat and my head instead of from deeper down in my chest.

More than that, she'd taken an interest in me as a human being, supporting me on my path. She celebrated my successes and commiserated about my struggles. We discussed my goals and aspirations, and she always cheered me on, encouraging me to tell my story – not only to her, but to the world.

She helped me to find not just my speech, but my voice.

* * *

I finish my tea and settle the bill. I stand up from my table and walk towards the door, calling back to the waitress as I leave: 'Thanks! And enjoy the rest of your day!'

There had been a time, not long before, when I'd been rendered silent. I had little that I felt was worth saying, and I did not feel like I deserved to be heard. Now, I am willing to engage. I have a story to tell, value to add, principles for which I have to stand up.

And the voice with which to do so.

Celebration

Day –46, 16 May 2015

I arrived at the restaurant at 7:29 p.m., characteristically punctual. I wore a fitted black dress bought specifically for the occasion, complemented by a pair of heeled black ankle boots and a lime-green clutch to break the monotony. It was a warm evening, though summer was just beginning to give way to winter. I strode across the open plaza, bustling with people as Melrose Arch usually was, and made my way towards the restaurant, a sprawling, multilevel affair. I greeted the waitress at the door, and asked for the table that I had reserved. The restaurant was packed with patrons, the background music inaudible behind the chatter of so many voices.

'Twenty people, ma'am?' the waitress asked.

It shocked me a bit to hear it. Twenty people, not counting the apologies. It seemed like an awfully big gathering, especially for someone like me. I had never thrown any kind of party in my own honour. Even my birthdays I'd tried to ignore.

But that had been the old me, who'd had neither a good reason to celebrate nor a desire to find one.

* * *

It was exactly one week since I'd resolved that I would no longer present as male except out of necessity. One week since the name on all of my online profiles had changed, the old photos had been taken down, and the new ones had been put up.

Presenting as male had become increasingly uncomfortable for me. Even in the company of people who knew the truth about

147

me, it had an effect on my mood. I'd be reserved and visibly restrained, my movements rigid, my back hunched. I'd speak reluctantly and, when I did, my speech would be laboured.

But in recent weeks, the intensity of my discomfort had grown relentlessly. It had come as a shock when friends had pointed out to me that it had become apparent to them. The more I grew into myself, the further I grew from 'him' and the less capable I became of maintaining the illusion.

As the weeks and months had passed, the barriers to my social transition had fallen. My facial hair, dark enough still to be visible beneath the surface of my skin even after the closest of shaves, had grown patchier with each session of laser therapy. My voice had become higher, breathier, lighter. The hair on my head had started to thicken and regrow, as the damage that testosterone had done to my scalp began to reverse.

I'd made the decision last Saturday morning. For a few weeks, I'd already been pruning my social media accounts – deleting old photos and tags, and removing as many references to my dead-name as I could. It had become painful to look at the old photos.

There'd been a knot in my stomach and a lump in my throat as I'd uploaded my new ones. My circles on social media had been carefully curated, and most of the people in them already knew. But in a world where our lives and our online existences are so intimately connected, there had been something momentous about making this 'Facebook-official'. Within moments, my phone had started ringing. Rose, my closest friend, calling to congratulate me, messages from my brother. More phone calls from friends. Likes and comments and messages wishing me well, saying it's about time, commending me for my courage, complimenting me on my looks.

The response had been overwhelming – it had felt, in that moment, as if the whole world approved. I'd smiled as tears had streamed from my eyes.

Freeing myself had not caused my world to implode.

* * *

As the waitress led me to my table, I was overcome with excitement, joy and pride – I had braved the Department of Home Affairs that morning. *A more-than-adequate cause for celebration*, I thought.

Already seated at the table were Rose, her husband Ben, her mother Trudy and her daughter Paige. Their faces lit up as I approached. They stood, embracing me one by one. I hugged Rose especially tightly. I'd met her in October, when I'd been on the verge of epiphany about my own gender identity. Since then, we'd grown steadily closer, and she'd become my closest friend. It was a momentous evening, and I was glad to have her with me.

My brother, whom I'd told two months ago, had never seen *me* in person. He walked into the restaurant with my mother a few minutes later. I flashed him a smile, and stood up to greet him. As he came closer, I saw that flicker in his eyes.

He finally understood. We embraced; I felt the warmth in his grip as he knowingly held his sister for the first time.

The table began to fill up with my friends. Leo, seated next to me, squeezed my hand as if to let me know that everything was okay. I didn't need to be reminded – I was consciously aware, in each moment, that everything was better than okay. My family and my closest friends, people who had stood by me through every hardship, surrounded me.

I'd had little experience in hosting gatherings, but I knew well enough that a good hostess circles the table and spends time chatting to each of her guests. As I did so, I was reminded how fortunate I was to have such wonderful, supportive people in my life: old friends who had known me for years, and new ones who had known me for months. Straight ones, gay ones, pansexual, cisgender, transgender, Jewish, Asian, Greek and Anglo-Saxon ones – a glorious amalgam of orientations and identities and cultures, all gathered in celebration with me.

I had a reason to celebrate, and was certain that I'd have many more.

Mother's Day

Day −42, 20 May 2015

It had been a quiet day at work. I sat at my desk, trying to clear some of the clutter that invariably accumulated on it. Stacks of X-ray reports and laboratory results were shuffled in amongst medical journals and promotional brochures for newly launched medicines. I willed the time to pass, counting the hours as they languished, my half-hearted attempts at tidying interrupted by the occasional patient. The practice knew no middle ground – it was either dreadfully quiet or ridiculously busy. Wednesdays, on which I only worked a half-day, seemed especially sluggish in their passing. This one was no exception.

My phone chimed. The message was from my mother, asking whether we had flu vaccines. She was in the area, and it would be convenient for her to drop in for a quick jab. The afternoons may still have been warm – hot, even – but the mornings and evenings were developing a sharp May chill to them. There was little doubt that winter was inexorably starting to set in. I quickly checked in with Judy before replying to my mother in the affirmative.

* * *

It amazed me how the dynamic of our relationship had changed. I had always struggled to relate to my mother. Years of physical separation had damaged the foundation on which our relation-ship had been built. My late father had instilled a deep sense of guilt and shame for wanting any kind of connection to her.

I had been conditioned to avoid that guilt and shame; to do so, I'd had to avoid her.

It had been more than seven years since I had been liberated from his tyrannical clutches, and nearly as many since his passing. I had grown to be independent and self-sufficient, but had still found it hard to communicate with my mother.

Coming out to her had changed everything. It had been over three months since I had first broached the subject of my gender identity with her, but she hadn't yet seen her daughter in person. I had been eagerly awaiting an opportunity to show her. It was the inevitable next step, one for which I'd long felt ready. I'd been sure that she would still have had some fears and uncertainties, and just as sure that seeing me in person would set her mind at ease.

The opportunity had finally presented itself about ten days earlier, on Mother's Day – a day that, in years gone by, had felt like a chore or an obligation. A day I used to dread, being a stinging reminder of our stilted relationship. A day of false pleasantries and artificial small talk.

I had spent the weekend visiting friends in Nelspruit whom I had not seen in a good three years. I'd driven down on the Saturday morning, an overnight bag with me that had not a single item of male clothing in it. It was the same Saturday on which I'd made the decision to start to present exclusively as female outside of work.

I'd been about halfway home late on the Sunday afternoon when I'd dialled her number.

'It's Mother's Day,' I'd said, 'and I have your gift. I'd love to see you.'

'Are you ...' she hesitated, 'Anastacia?'

'I'm *always* Anastacia,' I replied.

I'd known what she'd been trying to ask me. She'd struggled to find the words, but she'd wanted to know whether to expect the *real* me, the one she had not yet met.

'You know what I mean,' she'd said. 'I'm asking if you're–'

'—dressed in girl clothes,' I'd interjected, letting her off the hook. 'Yes, I am. Outside of work, I always am now. And I think you need to get used to that sooner rather than later.'

'Well, I'm home. Drop by whenever,' she'd replied.

The drive between Nelspruit and Johannesburg was long – more than three hundred kilometres – but it was peaceful. I'd become well acquainted with it during the years I'd worked in Mpumalanga. I had not travelled the road for three years, but had recalled every twist and turn. I'd gazed in awe, as I'd always done, at the beautiful mountainous landscape that stretched off to the horizon. I'd remembered that it always used to make me feel very small in comparison, and had noted with interest that this time, that sensation had been strangely absent.

Soon, the highway behind me, I'd approached my mother's townhouse. I had a set of keys, so I could let myself in. I had half expected her to be sitting in the lounge, staring at the entranceway, awaiting my arrival, but she'd been upstairs.

'Mom!' I'd called out. 'I'm here!'

I'd heard her footsteps on the stairs from where I'd stood in the middle of the living room's white tiled floor, supremely calm.

I'd been dressed in skinny jeans and a pair of brown knee-high boots. A fitted pink T-shirt had hugged my torso. Long, brown hair had framed my face, and I'd worn a pair of thick-rimmed plastic glasses, a studded bracelet on my wrist and rings on my fingers. I'd painted my nails metallic denim blue.

My mother had emerged from the stairwell and I'd spun around to greet her.

She'd stood silent for a moment as I'd walked up to her.

'You're ... gorgeous,' she'd stammered. 'Beautiful.'

'Don't look so surprised,' I'd answered softly, with a gentle smile.

'Turn around?' she'd asked.

I'd swivelled slowly on my heel.

'It just ... fits,' she'd said, tears forming in her eyes. 'It really just fits.'

'I know,' I'd whispered as I'd hugged her.

The embrace had been tighter than any I could remember since my childhood.

'Ana. You're my daughter. My beautiful daughter.'

We'd sat together in her living room, as we had done three months earlier when I had first told her. But this time, it was *me* who'd sat across from her.

She'd recognised almost immediately the difference in me: not just the clothes, or the make-up, but everything. She could see that an immense weight had been lifted from my shoulders. It had brought her to tears, but they'd been joyous ones.

Reunited, at last, with her child.

* * *

I had been busy with another patient when my mother arrived at the rooms. She waited in the reception area until my patient had left, then knocked on my office door to greet me.

'Come in,' I said.

The door slowly opened, and she froze for a moment as she saw me.

'I didn't recognise you,' she said.

It had only been a week and a half since she'd first seen me presenting authentically. Since then, I'd stopped in for a visit or two, and she'd been at my celebration dinner four days ago.

'I know,' I answered thoughtfully. 'I don't recognise myself either.'

Misconceptions

Day −36, 26 May 2015

'So, do you like boys, then?' Emily had asked.

'Couldn't you rather just have been gay?' my mother had asked.

'I'm open-minded. I just want you to be happy,' Zach had said when I'd told him.

'How do you know?' Leo had responded.

I'd become fairly used to telling people that I was transgender. After coming out to friends and family, I'd never gone to great lengths to hide my identity. As time passed, however, I began to notice a few patterns in the questions people would ask me, especially if they'd known me before my transition.

People seemed unable to resist the temptation to ask about my sexuality. Depending on who I was talking to, and the mood I was in at the time, I'd either brush off the question entirely or launch into a patient and lengthy explanation of the differences between assigned sex at birth, gender identity, gender expression and sexual orientation.

I'd go to pains, firstly, to reassure my audience that there was no need to feel guilty about having an incomplete understanding of these words and the concepts that they represented. They're not the kind of things that schools and universities educate us about, a tide that was changing slowly, at best.

I'd go on to explain that my sexual orientation was more about *them* than about *me*. It didn't relate to my gender at all, but rather to the gender of people to whom I experienced attraction. Terms like 'heterosexual' and 'homosexual' form a fallacious relationship between gender identity and attraction.

My gender identity, on the other hand, was an innate sense of who I was – man, or woman, or neither, unrelated to my sexual orientation, and not determined by the sex assigned to me at birth. The disparity between my assigned sex and my gender identity was the source of my dysphoria.

It had all been confusing to me at first, too. The existence of the phrases and identifiers, though they might not always have fitted perfectly, helped me to understand that I was not abnormal – I was just a different kind of normal.

Often, when coming out to people who had always related to me as a man, I'd need to explain the implications of my being gender dysphoric. Sometimes I would have to spell out that it meant that I did not identify in any way with my biological maleness, that I'd fallen victim to some manufacturing error that had taken place when I was a foetus. That trying to relate to the world around me as a man was alien and frustrating.

After I came out, people would frequently tell me that they thought me brave or courageous, or that they were proud of me. I always felt that the praise was undeserved. I had no choice in the matter of my identity; the only choice I had was how I would handle it. Even then, it was not much of a choice. To try to continue living life pretending to be a man was not survivable – of this I was certain. But I didn't feel like I deserved any praise for following my path.

As time went by, and I decided that I would live openly and make the story of my journey heard, words like 'courageous' became easier to reconcile. Taking the journey itself was no act of bravery, but talking about it was.

Another common response to my disclosure was, 'I am openminded.' I struggled to wrap my head around the fact that anyone should need to be open-minded not to take issue with another person's gender identity. When I'd heard it from those close to me, I was sure I'd understood what they had meant to say: 'I recognise that because of who you are, and the prejudice and intolerance inherent in the world, you are faced with adversity, and you must have been conditioned to be afraid of rejection. And I want you to know that you will face no such rejection from me.'

One would never respond to disclosures such as 'I'm short-sighted', 'I was born with a leaky heart valve', 'I've had red hair since I was a child' or 'I'm left-handed' by saying, 'Don't worry, I'm open-minded.' Some of these may be departures from what is common, but none of them is a choice. I did not choose my gender identity. My dysphoria caused me distress. Left unchecked, it would have killed me. My 'condition' was uncommon, but not abnormal. Nor was it an illness.

Why would anyone need to be open-minded to accept that?

The last question that came up fairly regularly was, 'When did you know?' My answer must've begun to sound very well rehearsed: 'It's something I've experienced my entire life, although I didn't always understand what it was.'

People seemed to expect some sort of lightbulb moment – a dramatic event in which the heavens opened up, and light shone down, and everything became clear. I hated to disappoint them, but the process was so gradual as to have been almost imperceptible.

It began with my inharmonious relationship with society and the role it had always wanted me to play. First, I realised where I didn't fit in – that I was different from other men in my behaviours and my thoughts. Next, a long stretch of time passed in which I ignored the implications of this difference. My deviation from accepted norms became my own normal, and I stopped being acutely conscious of just how divergent I was. Then, I began – slowly – to feel my way out, trying for the first time to find what *did* fit for me instead of what didn't. As I stripped away the fabricated mannerisms and behaviours that I'd sub-consciously embraced, I started to discover who I was. When I stopped disguising how I spoke, I found that it was soft and gentle, with instinctive inflections and prosody. When I stopped holding them down, my hands would flit about as I talked. I stopped reminding myself to try to sit in a manly way when I caught myself crossing my legs at the knee and sitting on the edge of the chair. I examined myself head to toe in the mirror and saw a slender waist, wide hips, tiny wrists, delicate hands and small feet.

On a day, I woke up certain of who I was, and of what I had to do. And on that day, whenever it may have been, not only was I sure, but I was unable to remember a time when I hadn't been.

Privilege

Day –32, 30 May 2015

I checked my shopping list as I strode down the passageway in the busy shopping centre.

Coffee.

Nutella.

Foundation, shade 125.

Hormone tablets.

Shampoo.

Aside from the hormones, it seemed like a typical list for a 29-year-old woman.

Shopping centres had been a source of anxiety for me, until recently. In the days when I used to present as male, I had always felt uncomfortable in them, as if I'd been on trial. I'd feel like I was being watched, even when no one was looking. Now, although I felt more comfortable, there were many occasions on which people were, in fact, looking. I'd become insecure and wonder what they were staring at – whether some constellation of physical features was giving away my history, perhaps.

The truth was that they were staring because I was a woman, and that's what people do to women in public. The men's eyes caress you without your consent, and the women's make silent judgements and comparisons.

Every time I needed to use a public restroom, I gave a silent word of thanks. My natural features lent themselves to femininity; I was what society expected of a woman. My gender expression – the way I dressed, acted and spoke – came naturally to me. I had always been binary. I wasn't trying to fit in with any set of standards – it just so happened that I did.

I didn't try to hide who I was. In conversation or on social media, my being trans was not a subject I shied away from. But here, in the crowded mall, no one knew that. Nor was it any of their business – which meant that I could go about my business in peace. If I needed the ladies' room, I didn't have to think twice about the consequences of entering it. Changing-room attendants did not give me a second glance. I was fortunate that my appearance and my physical features were such that I'd never had to face indignities or answer awkward questions. Even my voice no longer betrayed me.

I did not take my good fortune for granted. I had heard countless stories from transgender friends and acquaintances about the abuse to which they'd been subjected, and of how they'd queue to use the disabled or family restrooms because they were too scared to go to any other.

The slurs and prejudice were real. Whereas neither I nor anyone in my circle had been subjected to physical violence, there was always the fear that it could happen. It happened routinely in other countries, and it happened in South Africa, more often in townships and rural villages. It could happen to us. For those whose identities lay outside the binary and who rejected the traditional interpretation of gender, even day-to-day life was a difficult prospect.

Being trans, especially visibly so, is dangerous. Often, it meant being shunned by friends, rejected by family and harassed on the street. Sometimes, it even meant being beaten up, raped or murdered.

I was unfortunate to live in a world that was so prescriptive about identities and bodies, but privileged to have been less affected by it on a personal level than many of the people I cared about. At one stage, I'd felt a degree of survivor guilt over how 'easy' it had been for me to fit in. A transgender life is never an easy life. But for all its challenges, perhaps mine was easier than it might have been.

Still, I dreamt of a world in which transgender people didn't have to pay a price for things they did not choose and could not control. A world whose rigid boundaries and expectations did not exist – where people did not need to dread the consequences of living an authentic life, or feel compelled by fear to fit in.

A world where we felt welcome.

Dating while trans

Day 21, 22 July 2015

I lie on the bed while Hayley, my laser therapist, applies cold gel to the left side of my jawline. I can feel the temperature of it, and that isn't very reassuring – it means that the anaesthetic cream that I had slathered on earlier that morning is beginning to wear off. She holds the laser hand-piece, shaped like a gun, to my jaw.

'So, what's dating like?' she asks.

Ping-ping-ping from the machine as it fires its pulses deep into the hair follicles beneath my pale skin. The sensation feels like a thousand pinpricks, all concentrated on a single spot. Even with the numbing cream and some strong painkillers, it is searing. I try not to flinch and dare not speak, worried that if I move, the machine could burn my tender flesh.

'I mean, who are you attracted to?' she continues. 'What's your orientation?'

The pinging stops, and she begins applying the icy gel to the next area of my face.

'I've spent a lot of time thinking about it,' I say, enjoying the brief respite from the hot, needling stabs, 'and although I'm not very sexual to start with, I think I'm pretty much gay.'

'So, you're into ...' She is tentative.

'Women,' I reply, brusquely.

'Oh yes. Of course.'

Ping-ping-ping.

* * *

Dating has never come easily to me. I blamed it on the fact that I'd been poorly socialised, that I'd grown up in isolation from my school friends and had never been able to attend social functions. The excuse was convenient – and maybe even true, at least to an extent. Probably more significant was that I'd never felt at home in my own body or comfortable with the roles and expectations that came with inhabiting it.

I had a string of unmitigated romantic failures in my young adulthood. I struggled to understand what I was doing wrong, but found it difficult to secure a first date and virtually impossible to have a second. I was shy, polite, probably too gentle for my own good. A hopeless romantic, never very physical, and unsure of myself – which must have shown.

I needed some time to recover from my relationship with Jennifer, whose infidelity had left a raw and painful wound. But as time passed, the anguish became less acute. Feeling more secure in who I was than ever before, I knew that it was time to learn anew how to flirt, date and build connections with new people.

I had no idea where to start.

Meeting new people is not easy, especially when one was rapidly approaching 30 and had a small circle of friends, many of whom were married with children. Clubs, bars and noisy parties had never been my haunts of choice; I did not imagine that this was about to change. Online dating seemed like the best avenue. I set up a profile. Reading through it before finalising it, I found it to be witty, poignant and, most of all, honest. I added a few photos that I thought were especially flattering, and sent it off into cyberspace.

There were so many things I had to consider that had never been an issue before. Disclosure was probably the most pressing concern. Prejudice was real, and I feared its power. I imagined forming a fledgling connection with someone only to have them cut contact upon finding out that I was trans. Worse yet, perhaps they'd think themselves victims of deception and react with violence. In theory, I knew it shouldn't make a difference which sex I'd been assigned at birth. In practice, I knew that my life may well depend on it.

I decided it was in my best interests to declare my identity on my profile. There was little to lose, I figured. After all, I was already out of the closet in the other spheres of my life. Given the uniqueness of my name, I was already fairly easy to track down on social media, where I was open about my identity. I felt no shame in being visible for who I was; being transgender did not define me, but it was part of me.

The problem, of course, is that being trans is a deal-breaker for many people. Just by existing, I challenged the notion that sex and gender were inextricably linked. Worse still, I blurred the boundaries of sexual orientation.

Straight men would struggle to understand that being with a transgender woman made them no less straight. Lesbian women would similarly wrestle with the idea that being attracted to me made them no less gay. Some would wonder what their friends or family would say, as if there were a great shame in dating a trans woman.

At the same time, I was trying to understand my own sexuality. I didn't recall being attracted to men at any point in my life. I did recall feeling threatened or intimidated by them. I wasn't sure if any of that had changed as I had come to know myself better. Although I'd never been highly driven by sexual desire, I had always found women more attractive, more approachable and easier to understand. I was willing to be open-minded, even though I had my misgivings.

Soon, I started receiving unsolicited messages from men.

Routinely, they lacked punctuation and were grammatically incorrect, and seldom exceeded a line or two. Some of them were horribly vulgar, moving straight to asking after my genitalia. Some of them just sent me unwelcome pictures of their own.

It didn't take long for me to remember why men made me feel threatened. Many of them viewed me as an object, believing that I owed some debt of gratitude for their having shown interest in me in the first place. Worse than that, by far, were the ones who fetishised me and my body. To these men, the 'chasers', my body was a fantasy – a way of living out their darkest and most shameful desires without making them question their fragile heterosexuality.

In fairness, the odd gentleman was respectful, polite and inoffensive; I searched for physical or intellectual attraction to men like these, but did not find it.

When it came to women, I sought out the ones who identified as lesbian, bisexual or pansexual. I received a few messages out of the blue from some of them, asking me if I'd like to chat. I imagine some of them must have not read my profile properly, as they simply cut off all contact after their initial communications. Of the few I approached, only a fraction replied, again with many of them disappearing after exchanging a message or two.

It was disheartening. Despite all the energy I'd expended and the pain I'd endured to transition, there were still certain qualities for which I longed. No amount of surgical expertise would ever allow me to bear children. I'd have no cramps and no bleeding, but I was inescapably infertile. Other surgical procedures may, ultimately, grant me some of the characteristics that should have been my birthright, but infertility was a painful sentence.

Part of me felt that I would always be 'defective', that the shortcomings of my genetics had rendered me unlovable. Who would want a woman who was engaged in a constant battle with her own body? One who could never bear children? Who was reliant on medical intervention for her continued existence? It took great focus to remind myself that many women – even cisgender ones – felt ill at ease in their own skins, were barren, or required ongoing medical treatment. None of these facts diminished my worth as a woman.

But it was all too easy to forget.

Even on the odd occasion that I did manage to strike up a lengthy and deep conversation with someone for whom my being transgender wasn't a problem, there were so many mis-understandings. One young girl asked me, on our first date, 'So, if you prefer girls and you're trans, why didn't you just stay a straight guy?'

It took me a few moments to gather my composure. Eventually, I calmly answered: 'You're a girl, and you prefer girls. So, why don't you transition and be a boy?'

She thought silently for a moment, before she nodded in understanding.

Sometimes, I wondered if it wasn't easier just to avoid all the explanations and make a point of trying to date other trans people only. People who could understand why I wasn't always at ease in my own body, why I may not be able, always, to be physical, to whom I didn't have to explain so much. But even then, there was the inherent risk that our own dysphoria and insecurities would each feed off the other's. I had a hard enough time supporting myself through bad spells of dysphoria, and I wondered if I'd have the strength to support someone else through theirs.

I did go on a few dates with a lovely trans man, a perfect gentle-man with a big heart. I wished I could have felt more attracted to him. I gave myself every chance, but it simply wasn't there. I wished I'd been able to give him more of myself, but I didn't know how to. And there's no amount of wishing that can force something to exist that doesn't want to exist in the first place.

As with my sense of self and my gender identity, my orienta-tion was innate and unchangeable. I tried to remind myself that I was free to feel attraction wherever I felt it, and not to hold myself accountable if I didn't.

I laughed for a moment, realising that I'd come to have the minority market cornered. Queer, Jewish, trans, demisexual and lesbian: people would be spoiled for choice as to the grounds on which they chose to discriminate against me.

I longed just to put any ideas of dating and romance behind me, but it was a difficult thing to do. Being comfortable with myself and secure in who I was for the first time, I felt I had so much love and compassion, and I longed to share it. Not just that, but my own body had begun to feel like home. Never before had I been able to enjoy any kind of physical intimacy – dysphoria had seen to that. But I found myself craving physical sensations, longing to know what the touch of another would feel like, inside skin that belonged to me. The idea was intoxicating and tempting.

Of course, not just any touch would do. It would have to be someone I trusted, someone in whose hands I knew I would be safe. Someone with a soft, gentle, considerate touch, one willing to stop at a moment's notice should the need arise. Someone who understood that while some of the bits may be incongruous, they may be able to give or receive pleasure if they were treated with the requisite tenderness.

I gave myself, on occasion, to daydreaming of such an encounter. Flesh pressed against flesh, soft and warm, small beads of sweat forming between bodies. A tender embrace and a gentle caress, sensual and playful. Tracts of skin, untouched for months, and so deeply changed under oestrogen's influence, yearning to be explored. Curves and mounds freshly grown, pleasing to the eye and doubly so to the touch. Bountiful hips and milky thighs, supple and limber, stretched out beneath eager fingertips.

I never let myself think for too long, and still I struggled to let go.

* * *

'It feels like a crime,' I say, as Hayley applies the next lot of gel.
'What?' she asks.
'Dating,' I answer. 'Dating while trans.'
She says nothing, and presses the hand-piece back against my flesh.
Ping-ping-ping.

Thriving

Day −26, 5 June 2015

I rang the buzzer at the gate that led to the psychiatrist's reception area. I wore a pair of denims with a dark wash, and a fitted black sweater with a scarf knotted around my neck. My nails were painted in a dark, shimmery purple, my slender fingers adorned with rings, and I wore a delicate bracelet on my left wrist – a far cry from the polo shirt and chinos I'd worn to my first visit, six months earlier.

The latch on the gate released. I tugged it open and strode down the corridor towards the reception desk. The receptionist greeted me. The first time I had come to these rooms, I had dreaded the encounter with the psychiatrist. On this occasion, it was dealing with the reception staff that I had been anxious about.

Knowing that they had me listed in their appointment book under my highly gendered deadname, I was concerned that I may have some explaining to do – or worse, that they may misgender me in front of other patients in the waiting room, referring to me as 'sir'.

On the way in, I had reminded myself that hundreds of patients walked through the reception area every month, that the odds of them remembering me were slim, and that their job was just to greet patients and receive payments. In my favour, the title of 'Dr' conveniently allowed me to escape the pigeonholes into which most honorifics would otherwise have lumped me.

I introduced myself in my most feminine voice, thanks to months of hard work with Michelle. I was to be Dr Ross's last appointment for the afternoon, so the receptionist had me settle the account at the outset, since she was likely to have left before I finished. She advised me to have a seat and help myself to a cup of dubious coffee while I waited.

As I sat down, I breathed a sigh of relief. The hardest part was over; I'd forgotten that most people were too preoccupied with themselves to pay attention to those around them.

* * *

Kevin Ross had been my first professional point of contact after I had come to the realisation that, for me, medical transition was a necessity. I had approached him based on several recommendations from trusted friends, and because I knew he had a special interest in matters related to gender. The fact is that I had never suffered from, or been diagnosed with, any psychiatric comorbidities – no depression, no anxiety disorders, no personality disorders, no psychoses, none of the typical conditions that psychiatrists are accustomed to treating. But gender dysphoria remains a psychiatric diagnosis, despite its not being treated with psychiatric medication or intervention. The psychiatrist is a gatekeeper – he or she is tasked with determining whether the patient is, indeed, gender dysphoric, and for making the appropriate referrals to those who will ultimately take responsibility for the patient's medical or surgical care.

The twisted reality is that it is the 'job' of the transgender patient to convince the psychiatrist that he or she merits that care. The burden of proof is ours to bear.

Six months ago, when I had first come to see Kevin, I had been a bit bewildered and confused – not by my identity, because even then I had known, without any doubt, that I was a woman, but by the prospect of transitioning. It would turn my life upside down, sowing chaos where order had once ruled. It would change my relationships, with myself and with everyone around me. It would change the way the world perceived me and alter, irrevocably, the way in which I navigated my reality.

168

It was terrifying, but even then I'd had no doubts that it was necessary. I may have been despondent at the time, but my survival instinct had remained very much intact.

Looking back on my first interaction with Kevin, I was sure I'd failed to convince him. I did not fit the pattern that he had come to expect from transgender patients. I was functional in my day-to-day life. I was financially secure, with a steady job. I had no history of attempts at self-harm or suicide. I dressed in clothes appropriate to a man, and I didn't come across as being 'queer'.

The concept is always hard to understand for people who have not experienced it for themselves. And Kevin, though I was sure he meant well, was a cisgender man. The range of experiences and identities that fall under the umbrella of transgender is astonishingly broad. Each of us is subject to our own unique set of social and psychological circumstances that influences and informs the ways in which we live: despite pervasive depictions that the media has perpetuated for decades, we do not have a single, shared narrative that validates our identities. Some of us felt from a young age that we were trapped in the wrong body, 'cross-dressed' as children, or suffered intense physical dysphoria that led us to self-harm. Many of us did not. Some of us have always known our truths; others took decades to figure it out. Pattern recognition is a flawed tool when the patterns themselves are so varied as not to be patterns at all.

Even in my childhood, I had known I didn't fit in. But more than that, I had known that it was in my interests to avoid attention. I knew, for example, that asking for Barbies instead of GI Joes would have resulted in uncomfortable consequences. I feigned disgust at anything that may have been considered 'girly', because that was the kind of behaviour I reasoned was to be expected of a typical boy. At school, I'd kept mostly to myself, using my intellect as a commodity. And as an adult, I continued to suppress the mannerisms and behaviours that I knew were not acceptable for someone read by society as male.

Survival techniques and camouflage – some conscious, some subconscious, but all subterfuge. I had spent years perfecting the craft, honing my ability to deceive.

Unsurprisingly, Kevin had not been convinced.

* * *

I sat in the waiting room for about fifteen minutes before he finally called me through.

He stared at me slack-jawed for a few moments before he spoke.

'Look at you!' he exclaimed. 'What a transformation!'

'I'm not pretending any more,' I said.

If ever there was any doubt, this exchange had convinced me – seeing is, indeed, believing. And, in the absence of seeing, often there is disbelief.

I had made the appointment because I'd come to think of Kevin more as a guidance counsellor than a psychiatrist. I'd need to leave my place of work soon and hoped that Kevin may be able to suggest new avenues in which my transgender identity and my paperwork would not prove to be problematic.

Of course, part of me also wanted him to see and believe. Not for any vindication on my part, but because I knew that I was not likely to be the last transgender patient he'd ever see. I hoped that seeing the real me would encourage him to rethink some of his preconceptions and re-examine some of his prejudices. And that maybe, someday far off in the future, another trans patient may have an easier time in his office because of it. Misconceptions about what it means to be transgender are deep-seated and abundant.

As I sat in Kevin's office, my life may not have been without adversity, but I was surviving. More than that, I was thriving. For the first time, I had begun to learn how to love the person I was. I sincerely hoped that he would see that.

Safe space

Day 27, 28 July 2015

I park in the driveway, balancing a stack of pizza boxes and a bottle of wine precariously as I climb out of the car. Rose stands in the doorway, smiling broadly, then rushes out to hug me.

I hug her back as best I can with full hands.

'I missed you,' she whispers into my ear, as I bury myself in her shoulder and her long red hair.

'I missed you more,' I answer.

She squeezes me a bit tighter, holding for a few moments before we reluctantly release each other.

It has been a few weeks since we last saw each other. Rose has been on holiday near the coast, and I have been in turmoil since I left my job. Life has an unwelcome habit of getting in the way.

The absence and the distance is always painful, but that pain is testament to the strength of our bond.

* * *

Shortly after the end of my relationship with Jennifer, Rose and I found each other through a social network on the Internet. We were both vulnerable at the time – she was recovering from the loss of her father.

I was especially making an effort to be more outgoing and forthright. We chatted for a few weeks online, sending messages back and forth. In one of my very early messages to her, I mentioned that I believed gender identity to be a spectrum, and that I was still trying to figure out where on that spectrum I fell. I breathed a sigh of relief to have put my struggle into words, and another when she reacted with compassion and not disgust.

As weeks passed, before we'd even met, not a day went by that we didn't speak to each other. Our witty, and often cynical, exchanges belied a growing concern and affection for each other. Already, she'd begun to feel like a kindred spirit.

I agreed to meet her on a whim. It was scarcely a week before my birthday, the first one I'd be spending alone in seven years. I felt fragile. I was not thinking highly of myself, and longed to distance myself from everything that I'd grown habituated to being. I wanted to do things that were out of character, things that were reckless and misguided.

Meeting someone I'd encountered on the Internet is the sort of thing I would generally have approached with caution. But when Rose suggested that I come to visit her while she was in hospital, I agreed without hesitation. Even as I'd walked up the stairs to her ward, I expected to feel anxious. Instead, I felt strangely calm.

In the time since that first impromptu meeting, she and I had grown ever closer. I'd grown to respect and admire her astonishing courage. She was fighting a chronic immune deficiency that necessitated frequent hospital admissions and regular treatment with intravenous antibodies, and she faced it with bravery and grace.

She was a wonderful mother to a daughter whom she treasured and prized above all else. She was guarded sometimes, and cynical, but her defences protected a tender, compassionate, loving essence. She didn't care what other people thought of her, and wasn't afraid to stand up to anyone who threatened those she loved. More than that, she learnt to let me in, to confide in me and to trust me, even when it made her feel exposed and vulnerable. She was just the sort of role model I needed.

Rose was one of the last people to see the side of me who pretended to be male, and one of the first to see the woman who blossomed from the shell left behind when I stopped. I grew into myself in front of her eyes. She watched as I found my feet, my voice, my poise. And she supported me every step of the way.

I was unused to reaching out to anyone, accustomed to handling hardship on my own. But Rose never made me feel threatened. I trusted her without reservation. I knew that if I called out, she'd drop everything in a heartbeat and come running.

When necessity demanded that I presented as male, Rose still treated me as the woman I knew I was. My appearance, my clothes and my voice had never been of consequence to her; she knew me as a person, and my value and my identity were independent of those superficial trappings. Even in golf shirts and chinos, to her I was still Staci.

She pointed out the ways in which my body had changed when I failed to notice, and she was never far away with a word of support or encouragement when I began to feel despondent. I'd come to feel like part of her family. Her mother, her husband and her daughter all treated me with the utmost respect and love and understanding. Their acceptance was overwhelming and, at first, disconcerting. But I appreciated how welcoming they were to me, and how at ease I felt in their home.

Rose became my safe space, my sanctuary when my load felt too heavy to bear. Her warm embrace was a bastion that sheltered me from prejudice, injustice and self-doubt. When we'd first met, she'd been naïve about many transgender issues – the correct terminology, the matter of pronouns, the concept of dysphoria, the process of transition. But she'd been willing to learn; more than that, she'd desperately wanted to learn. The interest she took in me and in the challenges that I faced moved me deeply. I was her friend, and if something was important to me it was, by extension, important to her.

She was a source of confidence and inspiration I could draw on when I needed to. Any time I found myself faced with a difficult situation, I'd spend a few moments thinking about how strongly she believed in me, and how I wanted to make her proud. She helped me to climb more mountains than I could count.

Occasionally, I wondered how she felt about the man I'd pretended to be in the very short time that she knew him. I wondered if she'd become attached to him, if she missed him, and if she felt a sense of loss when he ceased to exist. I knew there were qualities of that persona that she'd loved and respected, and I accepted that perhaps it had been hard for her to let the idea of him go, even though he had never been real.

But I never doubted, for a single moment, that she wanted her friend to be free.

* * *

It still shocks me to think that Rose and I met not even ten months ago.

In many ways, my relationship with her is symbolic of my relationship with the world. I've gone from being awkward and shut off to confident, relaxed and open. I met Rose when I was scared of the world and mistrustful of myself. Since then, I've learnt to treat myself with love and respect, and to believe that I have a place within the world instead of just satisfying myself with watching from the sidelines.

She leads me inside, and I head for the kitchen, placing the wine and the pizza on the counter. We hug again.

'I missed you,' I whisper this time, as I hold her as tightly as I can.

'I missed you more,' she answers.

Promises

Day −20, 11 June 2015

Steam engulfed the bathroom as I emerged from the shower. It had already been a few months since I'd begun setting the alarm clock fifteen minutes earlier to give me enough time to shave what little stubble still insisted on sprouting while I slept. It had become progressively more difficult to leave my warm bed as winter had set in, but I forced myself nonetheless – it was less uncomfortable to endure the cold than it was to tolerate the unwanted hair for any longer than was necessary. I longed for the morning I'd wake up and run my fingers across smooth, hairless cheeks.

But that was still a few sessions of laser hair removal away. In the meanwhile, I had resigned myself to the necessity of scraping away at my face with a blade at least once a day. The nicks and the cuts hurt far less than the hair.

*   *   *

My mornings had become almost ritualistic. I'd wake up at the same time every day, stumble to the coffee machine, shower, shave, brush my teeth, get dressed. The more routine it was, the less I had to think about it.

More than a month before, I'd made the decision that I was no longer prepared to present as male in any setting aside from work. All my friends knew me as I was meant to be – the moody dissembler had been replaced by a vivacious, confident woman. I still had commitments to my job and my employer, but the pretence was becoming harder to maintain. Every morning,

I had to pack away my identity carefully; at the end of each weekend, I'd sit down and scrub my nails, removing whichever polish had adorned them.

It's just nail polish, I'd try to remind myself.

At work, mothers gently coaxed their children to allow the 'nice man' to examine them. Men would greet me with 'howzit, *boet*'; women would ask me for referrals to gynaecologists because they were uncomfortable having me perform their pap smears. Every script and medical certificate, signed with my deadname in thick, black ink.

Patients would often ask me what was wrong; pretending to be someone else was exhausting. Every sideways glance at my reflection in the mirror betrayed me, and made me feel like I'd betrayed myself.

Medicine, for me, had always been more about compassion and interpersonal relations than laboratory results and diagnostic tests. The true skill in being a doctor was the ability to communicate with and relate to individuals, to see them as people instead of flesh, bone, sinews and blood. It was often painful. But, like an abusive partner, medicine tempered the heartache with just enough rewarding and fulfilling moments. It expertly toyed with my emotions, keeping me on the line and refusing to allow me to leave. Not that I wanted to; I loved what I did and knew I was good at it. I hated knowing that gender was impairing my ability as a doctor and a caregiver.

Sitting behind my desk, wearing *his* uniform and answering to *his* name, I occasionally allowed myself to daydream about what it would be like to interact with my patients unfettered by falsehoods. My knowledge and skills as a clinician were independent of my gender identity. Transitioning had not undone the years of studying that had shaped me as a doctor, or my ability to handle lab results and diagnostic tests, palpate flesh, manipulate bone, stitch sinews, or draw blood. But the communication, the discourse, the connection between carer and patient – freed from the grip of maleness, it could finally be sincere. Brandishing the pink stethoscope of my daydreams between manicured fingers, I enjoyed my new-found freedom. I no longer had to suppress my emotions or hide my compassion.

It was a dream with which I had to part every time the phone rang or there was a knock on my office door.

Perhaps most frustrating of all were the few patients who had been referred to me who were trans themselves. Of course, I loved to treat them, to see the relief on their faces when they realised they were not on trial and the surprise when they recognised that I knew more about gender than they had expected. To see the elation they experienced as their hormone therapy gently began to reshape their bodies.

I longed to say, 'I know what you're going through. I've been there.'

* * *

Blood mixed with shaving cream spiralled the basin, succumbing to gravity's pull as I held the razor underneath the running tap. I splashed cold water onto my face, the skin on my cheeks feeling tight as I clenched my jaw. I ran my fingertips across my jawline, still red from the razor, feeling for the prickle of stubble. Even if I couldn't feel it, I still imagined that I could see the blue-black hue of its roots.

I buttoned up my shirt and pulled up my chinos, feeling them hug my hips tightly enough to hurt. I fastened my belt to secure the slack they left around my waist. Over, under, up, around and through – muscle memory helped me to knot the tie I'd yanked from the wardrobe.

I looked at the girl in the mirror, hidden beneath ill-fitting garments. She looked back, her brown-eyed gaze tearing into me. I'd promised myself I wouldn't cry that day. I grasped for a tissue and dabbed my eyes, consoling myself: in life, there are always some promises that just can't be kept.

Agents of the dispensary

Day 48, 18 August 2015

The queue at the dispensary, fortunately, is not a lengthy one. In front of me stands an elderly lady propped up by a Zimmer frame and, in front of her, a young couple. I have already picked up the few groceries I needed at the mall; the pharmacy is my last stop before I head home.

It is the sixth time I've come to collect my medicines since starting hormone replacement therapy. Many of my body's changes had been gradual, almost imperceptible for someone who looked at herself in the mirror daily. Friends and family were often the first to point them out to me, but looking back at old photographs, the differences are unmistakable.

I'd never had the most masculine of features, fortunately. A narrow waist and wider hips meant I'd always had trouble finding jeans in the men's section. My size-eight feet are large for a woman, but not abnormally so. I am able to buy shoes in any mainstream shop. Better yet, my size is seldom sold out.

My five-foot-eight frame means I'd have made a good flight attendant. In heels, I am quite striking, but the attention is flattering rather than embarrassing. My hands are delicate and small, my fingers long and slender. Over the years, patients, colleagues and friends had often commented on them. I'd become used to remarks about how gentle and dainty they are.

Six months of hormone therapy later, and I have begun to look like myself. Most of my body hair has turned to peach fuzz. My hips and my backside have filled out even further, and my waist has become narrower. My arms, once covered in muscle cultivated in an attempt to fit in, have begun to shrink and atrophy.

My face has softened, my cheeks are filling out and my skin is growing smoother and more supple. My nipples have recently begun to ache as breasts have started blossoming beneath them.

My hair has thickened and is steadily growing longer, having not been shorn in several months. My freshly pierced ears sport delicate floral studs while they heal. Pleasing curves replace straight lines, and my nails have grown out.

I feel at ease having the right balance of hormones coursing through my veins.

I recall the first time I'd filled my prescription, when the pharmacist had assumed it was for a wife I didn't have. Human beings have a tendency to fill in the blanks, to try to make sense of the unknown or the difficult-to-understand. The pharmacist had created a narrative to alleviate his uncertainty.

'Cash or medical aid?' he'd asked

'Cash,' I'd answered, and had snatched the parcel away from him as quickly as I could. I'd hurried towards the cashier, overcome with the irrational fear of a member of the Dispensary Police leaping over the counter, chasing after me, tackling me to the ground and wrestling the medications from my grip, finding me guilty of the crime of being in possession of oestrogen.

The pharmacist calls me to the counter, breaking my reverie. She is an Indian woman, a few years older than me. I remember her helping me before, a few months earlier. I'm sure she doesn't recognise me now.

We greet each other politely.

'How can I help you, ma'am?' she asks with a smile.

'I need to pick up my repeat script,' I say, handing her my customer card.

She rattles off the names of my medicines and I nod after each one. She doesn't seem in the least bit concerned about the name attached to the prescription.

'Just a minute,' she says, disappearing into the back room.

A few minutes later, she returns. 'Cash or medical aid?' she asks.

'Cash,' I reply.

She hands me the parcel.

'Thanks!' I say, as I take it from her gently. 'Enjoy the rest of your day!'

'You too!' she offers.

I stroll to the cashier, confident that no agents of the dispensary are in pursuit.

Anathema

Day −16, 15 June 2015

I entered the building marked 'Faculty of Health Sciences', and made my way to the security guard seated behind the reception desk to sign in. From the outside, the building had not looked terribly impressive, but inside it glistened – polished-tile floors, frosted glass and stainless steel finishes. It was far more opulent than I had expected.

I filled out the security register and all the intimate details it requested – name, ID number, vehicle registration, telephone number, reason for visit. I don't recall, but think I may even have been required to give my shoe size. I spent a moment wondering about the fate of these registers once they were full, and all the names and ID numbers inside them – the sort of information that could be sold on the black market for a tidy profit. I reminded myself that it didn't matter – my ID number would be changing in a few months in any event. I made my way to the lifts.

The Department of Family Medicine was my destination. As the lift doors opened, I stepped into the corridor. There were no signposts, neither on the walls nor on the doorways that led from the passageway. The entire floor seemed deserted. I glanced at the time – quarter to three. Perhaps family physicians did not work afternoons.

I chose a doorway and walked through it hesitantly, following a passageway that eventually led to me a reception desk. A note on the counter read 'Out of Office', as if that much wasn't clear already. I sat down on a couch in the corner of the reception area, checking my calendar to make sure I hadn't confused my dates.

I was still a few minutes early for my appointment. I was

to meet with one of the senior professors in the department, a woman who was involved with the university's support programme for LGBT students. I'd sent her an e-mail a few weeks before to introduce myself, and she had eventually responded. She'd seemed interested in my story and eager to help. I'd been told by friends who knew her personally that she tended to be a little unreliable, particularly in terms of keeping appointments, but that her heart was in the right place.

I had known for some time that, sooner or later, I would need to leave the private practice where I had been employed. I had flirted with the idea of opening my own practice, but that had seemed untenable at the time. As a doctor, most of what I did was tied, in some way, to my legal name. Every prescription I wrote had to be signed, and needed to bear the name under which I was registered with the health professions council. Until Home Affairs had processed the changes for which I had applied, that name was my deadname.

In addition to these bureaucratic difficulties, I recognised that perhaps I was not ready to bear the strain that would undoubtedly come with opening a new business. Transition was a stressful enough process – trying to grow a medical practice from scratch at the same time seemed almost suicidal. Of course, that was my long-term goal: to open a cosy little clinic somewhere, where patients of all genders, sexualities, races, ages and lifestyles would be welcome. Where they could seek medical care without prejudice. Where they would know that their doctor was a human being herself, one to whom they could relate, instead of some unapproachable, white-bearded demigod who would dictate to them what was to happen to their bodies.

The idea of my dream clinic made my heart swell with hope. I had no doubt that I would pursue it when the time was right.

But for now, I had decided to pursue more practical avenues. I had determined that by working in a state-run clinic or hospital, I'd be able to practise under the auspices of the supervising department rather than under my own name. The only challenge would be the job interview – not because my skills were inadequate, but because I'd have to answer questions about the name on my medical degree and the photograph on my identity document.

I had given the matter ample thought, and concluded that a job interview would necessitate 'outing' myself to the interviewers. I knew that the medical establishment, particularly in academic departments, tended to be closed-minded and old-fashioned. Despite the fact that, for many years, female medical students had vastly outnumbered male ones, senior academic positions still resembled an old boys' club.

The idea of sitting in front of a panel of conservative old men, set in their ways and entrenched in their prejudices, filled me with dread. When I'd been a student, some of my lecturers had been men like these. I envisioned the potential tirade of transphobic and homophobic slurs.

I determined that my best prospect was to find sympathetic individuals inside the different academic departments that I was considering, people who would be able to advise me about transgender-friendly career prospects in those departments.

I glanced again at the time. It was just after three o'clock. I heard the lift doors open in the corridor; moments later, a short woman with grey, curly hair and small, rimless spectacles balanced on the tip of her nose came bounding through the door.

'Anastacia?' She was out of breath.

'Yes,' I answered as she gently took my hand in greeting.

'Sorry to keep you! Come through to my office,' she said, leading me down another corridor.

She fumbled with the key for a few moments before throwing the door open.

This must have been the corner office. It was a large room, home to a desk, a small conference table and a couple of couches. Boxes were strewn around the floor, and the bookcases that lined the walls were untidy. The outward-facing side was entirely glass, affording a panoramic view of the city that stretched out below.

She pointed me towards the couch, and I sat gingerly.

Susan was eccentric and energetic. She spoke with an unmistakable accent that betrayed her years spent working and training in America and Canada. She'd been involved in a variety of community health and human rights projects over the years. She seemed like just the sort of person who would be able to help.

She sat down next to me and, after apologising for the state of her office, quizzed me about my background and upbringing. She asked about my childhood, my parents, my romantic relationships. I was touched by the interest she showed. She was a family physician through and through – not only interested in the presenting problem, but in an individual's context. It was reassuring. Clearly, she thought of me as a human being, not a walking, gender-dysphoric medical degree.

Eventually, she addressed my career. I told her that in the past, I'd toyed with the idea of working in a surgical department. The thought of working long nights several times a week and running myself into the ground, leaving no time for friends or family, had been appealing at one point. But that was a time when I hadn't cared much for myself. I'd had few friendships, and my relationships with my family had been strained. It was just the sort of avenue through which my self-loathing could have been expressed.

But transition had changed my outlook. I no longer wanted to martyr myself on the altar of thankless, unending labour, burnout and depression. I wanted a job that would allow me to look after myself, so that I could look after others. I wanted to be well adjusted, and well rested, with enough time and space outside of work to pursue other interests. I wanted to be the best doctor I could be, and had come to understand that the way to achieve this was through self-care rather than self-sacrifice.

I told her that I'd identified my true calling: I had found a passion for primary care. Having been a patient myself, I had experienced first hand some of the prejudice that comes with belonging to a minority group. I wanted to be a safe space for patients, where they would not be judged or persecuted for who they were.

Her gaze was wistful as she looked at me a few moments. It was clear that what I'd said had resonated with her, but at the same time it had awoken within her some kind of sadness or regret. I waited for her to speak.

'I don't think Family Medicine is the place for you,' she said, her voice softer than it had been before.

I waited.

'I understand what you want to do, and I think it's amazing. It's just the kind of thing that I have a passion for,' she said. 'In fact, I used to do something very similar in the US. But, South Africa still has a long way to go. And this department ...'

'What about it?' I asked.

'A lot of the consultants are very ... conservative. Traditional types, churchgoers. Family men. Their values are old-fashioned. I don't think they'd be able to accept you. Perhaps you'd be better suited to a department like Psychiatry, where they should be more progressive?'

Her answer didn't shock me. Just ten days ago, I had gone to see Kevin. In addition to the private practice he ran, he was a consultant for the university's Psychiatry unit. He'd said to me in no uncertain terms that, being on the inside, he knew that the department was not ready to work with a transgender doctor. The irony had not been lost on me. He'd suggested I try Family Medicine instead.

Every department, every consultant, every professor – they had all been sympathetic and understanding. They'd all been very willing to put me in touch with someone else they knew who may be able to help. They threw words like 'liberal', 'open-minded' and 'accepting' around because, in their minds, there was something about me that required liberality, open-mindedness and acceptance. I was different, and that difference was so inherently distasteful that I needed some sort of special dispensation to be regarded as acceptable.

Doctors liked things to be cut and dried and to fit into neat little boxes. They wanted people and bodies to be male or female, and anything in between was a cause of great distress. I thought back to my years as a student, remembering being taught that a child born with ambiguous genitalia is a medical emergency. The lecturer was talking about intersex conditions, of which there is a wide variety. Of the multitude, only one condition is life threatening – for metabolic reasons, not because of the intersex anatomy. Nonetheless, doctors still fly into a panic if they can't immediately determine a newborn child as unequivocally male or female. They coerce the parents of that child to agree to unnecessary surgery – genital mutilation – to make the child's genitalia more fully resemble typical anatomy. These procedures are costly, and not without complications, but they make the doctors feel more comfortable. Often, they will tell the parents to raise the child as whichever gender the doctors have chosen for it, and to keep the surgical intervention a secret from the child. Many of the children subjected to these operations grow up with intense dysphoria, and some even choose to transition. Those who do learn of the barbaric practices to which they were subjected are often angry and resentful. Yet knowing that the lines between male and female can never be crossed makes doctors feel more comfortable.

To doctors like these, I was anathema.

I didn't know my chromosome complement, or which internal reproductive anatomy I actually possessed. But, as far as I know, at birth I looked typical enough to have been assigned male. And yet, here I was, crossing those uncrossable lines.

Susan offered to circulate my CV on the off chance that an opportunity may present itself. She was genuinely apologetic that she could not do more for me. But I understood why her hands were tied.

I thanked her for her time, and made my way out. As I drove

off, I wondered just what it was about me that made people so insecure. I had never struck myself as being particularly scary, but evidently I had the white-bearded men shaking in their lab coats.

Dogma

Day −5, 26 June 2015

I sat at a small table in the middle of the cramped coffee shop. It was busier than I'd expected it to be on a Friday afternoon. Being a kosher venue, most of its regular patrons were religious Jews, and Friday afternoons were usually spent preparing for the onset of Shabbos. I realised I'd been fortunate to find a table.

I was to meet with Rabbi Schmidt, a South African expatriate who occasionally visited his former home country. My aunt had arranged the meeting. She was religious; though she cared for me deeply, it seemed she had struggled to understand the concept of my transition within the framework of religion. A few days earlier, she called me to say that she had met with a rabbi who had helped her to make peace with the issues that had been worrying her.

* * *

The religious school I attended dedicated much of the day to Jewish education, but my home was secular. As a young child, that conflict weighed heavily upon me. I had always felt a longing to be part of the Jewish community, but my secular home life made me an outsider to my classmates.

As I'd grown up, the dynamic had become even more confusing to me. I'd fulfilled certain observances, unsure of whether I'd done so out of habit or belief. The important fast days, certain dietary restrictions, the observance of Passover – they felt unshakable to me, so I complied with them, even if I didn't understand why. At the same time, I could never be regarded as properly observant – I'd not been devoid of faith, but had not been fully compliant with the demands that it had made.

On occasion I'd attend synagogue on a Friday evening or a religious holiday, and when I did so, I was inevitably overcome with confusing emotions. Synagogue afforded me a window into the community, to see the connection that its members shared and even to feel it myself for a little while. But I felt like an impostor.

I had been conditioned by my education not to question the religious texts. Once I'd admitted to myself that I was transgender, everything became more difficult. I routinely declined invitations to religious holidays or Shabbos dinners. If I couldn't find an adequate excuse, or I felt too guilty about rejecting so many invitations, I'd find myself standing in the synagogue feeling more uncomfortable than ever in my suit and tie. My very presence was deceitful, a heavy burden on my shoulders.

As I started to understand my identity, I also trusted my values more. I admitted to myself that some of the contents of the religious texts were disturbing – that I could not reconcile my own principles with what they seemed to say. Whether they were allegorical, figurative, or historical remnant made no difference – I could make no peace with them on any level.

I wondered how I had ever been able to make excuses for the sexism that seemed inherent to my faith. 'Blessed are You, Lord our God, Ruler of the Universe, Who has not made me a woman' is a prayer that men recite daily, testament to the idea that the feminine is subordinate to the masculine.

Judaism's views on gender dysphoria were no comfort to me. Authorities held different views on the matter, and many ignored it altogether. Some of them ruled that biology was irrefutable, and that to try to shift from one's assignment at birth was immoral, some sort of sin. Some even viewed gender-affirming procedures as a kind of suicide, unforgivable and unacceptable in the extreme. Even the few who recognised that transition may confer a change in gender status under Jewish law were insensitive, largely, to the process of transition itself. They minimised the journey and all of its nuances to a simple question of genital surgery – if it has been performed, then the person's gender has changed. Until that point, a transgender woman remains a man in the eyes of Jewish law, even if she has lived, presented, and been treated by the rest of the world as a woman for years. This reduced all of my experiences, all of my emotions, every single challenging step on this journey that would last for the rest of my life, to a surgeon and his or her knife.

To reduce a transgender life to a single surgical procedure is disrespectful and insensitive. Our lives are a constant struggle for acknowledgement and acceptance, so much more than a one-off encounter with a scalpel and a handful of stitches.

We are people, not genitalia, not secondary sexual characteristics. We are children and parents and siblings, we are friends and lovers. Our experiences and our circumstances are vast and varied. For many of us, the journey involves trying to liberate ourselves from the regulations that society imposes on our bodies so that we can live in them without pain or distress. Replacing one set of prescriptions with another is not liberation – it's just a different kind of servitude.

When word about my transition began to spread, predominantly in the Jewish community, I knew I was being talked about. Certainly, there were unsavoury comments. It's a sad reality that small communities often sustain themselves on gossip and scandal, the more salacious the better. My reality and the details of my transition were, in fact, quite mundane, but gossip does not let itself be hampered by concepts as inconsequential as the truth.

* * *

I was curious to hear what the rabbi would have to say. I had always had a great deal of affection for my aunt, and I knew those feelings were reciprocated. She cared about me and my well-being, and I trusted her recommendations.

In my mind, I had all but divorced myself from organised religion. I'd long stopped making excuses for the dogma that I often found cruel and barbaric, and had distanced myself from the community that perpetrated abuses in its name. Perhaps there still lived within me the hope that I may, one day, find some way to resolve this schism with the religion of my upbringing. But the community did not know where to put me.

I caught sight of the rabbi entering the coffee shop, and waved to get his attention. He shuffled over and took the seat across from me at the cramped table. The waitress approached us to take our orders. I ordered a coffee; the rabbi declined. He shifted uncomfortably in his seat as he looked at me.

I didn't know what to expect from this meeting. I'd been told that Rabbi Schmidt was knowledgeable and sensitive about transgender issues. I did not doubt that the man was compassionate and erudite, a great scholar of scripture. Nonetheless, he seemed uncomfortable with my presence, and unwilling even to speak.

He stared at me expectantly. I was lost for a few moments, unsure as to what I was meant to say.

'Thank you for taking the time to meet me,' I offered eventually.

He nodded, and continued to stare.

'I really appreciate that you have helped my aunt come to terms with this,' I said, trying to establish some kind of rapport.

'It's my pleasure,' he responded at last.

Silence again.

'I've mostly come to terms with who I am, and the journey I have to take,' I said, growing impatient, 'but I do struggle to reconcile this with the faith with which I grew up.'

He thought for a few moments before he spoke again.

'It is what it is, and you must live the way you need to. Be

191

careful. My blessing for you is that you should find your way.'

The experience was jarring. Our conversation, brief as it was, was laboured. I wondered what made the theoretical concept of a transgender person palatable, but the reality of meeting one so unnerving. I felt insecurity's familiar pang, the anguish that came with the realisation that something about me was intrinsically wrong.

Having given me his deliberately ambiguous blessing, he made his exit at the first opportunity he had. I didn't begrudge his doing so. I settled the bill and left the coffee shop shaken.

Later that evening, while I was no doubt a point of debate at many a Shabbos table, I began to consider alternative explanations. It had been proven to me, with no uncertainty, that religion and I were at odds. My encounter with the rabbi had erased whichever doubts I may still have harboured. I assumed that the problem lay with me – that I was unworthy because of my inherent qualities and my identity.

I was still unsure about which place, if any, I had within the structure of organised religion. But I knew that it would be wrong to allow that uncertainty to rattle my self-confidence. If my identity rendered me objectionable, in spite of my character, then the problem was with religion, not with me.

I had always considered myself to have faith in providence. Call it what you will – god, goddess, kismet, *anima mundi*, karma – the name was less important than the idea behind it. I existed as I did not by chance, but for a reason. The mismatch between my body and my mind was deliberate, as was the journey I needed to take to remedy it. The experiences I had endured and the perspectives I had gained, and would continue to gain, throughout this process had contributed to my worth as an individual and as a woman.

There was nothing shameful about that.

Sobriquet

Day 30, 31 July 2015

I walk into the nail salon, and approach the reception desk.

The lady behind the counter smiles and greets me.

'I'm here for my appointment,' I say, 'at three o'clock.'

'Yes, of course,' she answers. 'What's your name?'

I smile contentedly for a moment, before answering, 'I'm Anastacia.'

* * *

It has been a good few months since I have introduced myself by any other name, but the way it feels rolling off my tongue is still novel. I love the way my name sounds as I speak it, and I love the way it feels. I love hearing it when others call me by it.

Names have a strange power. They are labels and descriptors, in a very simple sense, but there is so much more to them than that. A name has, wrapped up inside it, some aspect of identity, some sense of self. Some names we allow to be public knowledge, while others we keep for private use, selectively deciding with whom we choose to trust them.

I never felt much attachment to my old name. It had, for a long time, felt foreign to me, even before I fully understood how incongruent it was with my gender identity. Even though I had been addressed by that name for close on three decades, it was a name that had never fitted. When people called me by it and, on occasion, I didn't respond by reflex, I'd take a moment and think, *Is that supposed to be me?*

I used to have a middle name, too. My first name I had to share with the world, but my middle name I kept a secret, sharing it with very few people and always reluctantly. There was nothing wrong with the name, but I was always uncomfortable sharing it. Perhaps because I'd never felt enough ownership of it to give the knowledge of it to others.

After admitting to myself that I had gender dysphoria and that I was transgender, my discomfort with my name became so much easier to understand. The name itself was highly gendered – it was a boy's name through and through. No wonder it had never felt like mine.

The name was a representation of all of the things I was not and had never been. Despite my nature and my character, the name carried with it certain associations and expectations, ones that were always inappropriate and uncomfortable.

When I still worked in Dr Katz's practice, so much of what I did was tied to my name, from prescriptions to office stationery. At that stage, even my Facebook profile still carried that name, though all of my closest friends had long stopped using it to refer to me. I took to using my initials in place of my first name. And, I was fortunate in that I could hide behind the gender-neutral title 'Dr'.

Using my initials and title were small concessions, but they were the best I could manage at the time. The small consolation of not having to write out my name in full was of little help when patients and practice staff still addressed me by it. Of course, they couldn't have known what it did to me.

And then there was the matter of my surname. My mother, who had divorced my father, had long since reverted to her maiden name. My half-brother Leo bore the surname of his own father. Mine was a yoke and a harness, binding me to and reminding me of my father's legacy of emotional abuse. I had no living relatives left who cared about me and who still used that surname.

There is a reason why we call our old names deadnames: they remind us of people we were forced to be, of the pieces of ourselves that we had to kill to become who we needed to be. Hearing and seeing them is often painful. Transition gave me a reason to cast off my deadnames, and the liberty to choose ones that resonated with who I was, as opposed to who everyone had willed me to be.

Retaining my surname would undoubtedly have been the more convenient option, as it would've allowed me to continue signing prescriptions under my surname and initial, but it was an avenue that I was never willing to consider. The choice was an easy one – I would abandon it and replace it with my mother's maiden name. I'd share a surname with the parent who loved and accepted me, rather than the one who had abused and disowned me.

Choosing my first name gave me a little more pause. I wanted a name that represented everything I was. I wanted a name that I owned, a name that I could be proud of. A name I loved to speak and hear, one I loved to see written down. A name that succeeded in every area in which the old one had failed me.

It is a privilege to be able to name oneself.

I chose the name Anastacia. I thought it was beautiful, the way it sounded and looked, and the way it felt when spoken. It did a poor job of blending in – it was a name that attracted attention, bold and arresting – a refreshing change for someone who had spent her whole life trying to avoid attention.

It held meaning, one that captured the essence of who I was and the path that had led me there, as well as the myriad of opportunities and possibilities that lay before me. It was a name I loved.

'Anastacia' means rebirth, resurrection, second chances and fresh beginnings. It means leaving the pain of the past behind, and starting anew, living a life the way it had been meant to be lived.

'Anastacia' means 'me'.

Break-up

Day 56, 26 August 2015

I walk to the kitchen and open the second drawer from the top, reaching in for the roll of refuse bags. I tear off three of them, the thick black plastic crackling beneath my fingertips. I make my way back to the bedroom and lay them out on the bed. I separate the first of them from the other two and shake it out a few times, filling it with air.

I set it on the floor, its mouth agape.

I throw open the doors of the cupboard that had once belonged to him. Staring back at me are his shirts, his trousers, his ties. Almost two months since any of them have been worn, but I still smell his scent on them every time I open those doors.

I take out a pile of his old T-shirts, and drop them into the thick bag's waiting mouth.

*   *   *

Having him around had been familiar, even comforting. I had grown reliant on him. He had never been a safe space for me, but I'd fallen into thinking that he was; co-dependency will do that to a person.

The realisation that an intimate relationship is abusive is never comfortable. It comes as a shock. The betrayal that went unrecognised for so long is bitter, and the shame of having allowed it to go unchecked weighs heavily.

My emotions were mixed. I was resentful of what he'd done to me but could not help feeling sorry for him. I felt as though I had been trapped under his thumb, made to feel inadequate, my self-esteem slowly but steadily wearing away as he'd gnawed at my insecurities. He'd made me feel ugly, misguided, stupid. Bit by bit, he'd torn me down: I was too fat, too sensitive, too weak.

Playing on my self-doubt, he'd made me shy away from social interactions. I'd neglected my friends, or pushed them away deliberately. They didn't deserve to be burdened with my trivial problems; besides, he had always been there to listen. I even isolated my own family, keeping them at a distance, shutting them out. I desperately wanted to maintain the facade that my life was idyllic.

He was the breadwinner, once. He used to give his all to that job, even at the expense of his own well-being. He was sacrificing himself, and I had no doubt that he believed in the idea of a greater good, of something bigger than himself.

He seldom allowed himself to smile, and I never saw him cry. Through heartbreak and loss and grief over missed opportunities, he shed not a single tear. I thought he'd been afraid that one drop may burst the dam.

His childhood had been a difficult one. He never spoke about it. He seemed not to remember much of it, and often said that he felt he'd been forced to grow up too fast. He had felt so much pressure to be as self-sufficient and independent as he could, even from a young age, that he'd sacrificed his childhood. His parents had set a poor example; no one had taught him how to love.

It would be unfair to suggest that he was not self-aware. He knew, without any doubt, that he had been damaged. Often he'd speak of how he longed to overcome the hurt, that he yearned to be better than it all.

With hindsight, the patterns were all so familiar. He had tried to survive in a world that he felt had never wanted him, tried to compensate for his flaws, tried to give, and give, and give and never to take. He wanted nothing more than to do some good, to make things easier for others.

But he had not held me back deliberately. He did not know

any better, of that I was sure. And though it may have been easier to blame him, to hold him accountable for all the suffering I'd endured during the time we'd been together, it wasn't fair to do so. I'd enabled him because of the safety and the comfort and the familiarity. And because I'd been afraid.

I knew all too well how it worked, and I knew it had to end. I rebuilt my own confidence, slowly. There were good days – nothing could stand in my way or bring me down. And there were bad days – I struggled to remind myself of my value. I learnt to celebrate every victory, no matter how small, and trained myself not to fixate on my failures.

Little by little, I regained my independence. I learnt to go out by myself and realised that nothing bad would happen to me if I did. I built strong friendships that did not crumble for no reason. I let people in, and wasn't shunned. Even my most closely guarded secrets were welcomed with compassion.

And the lies became visible for what they had always been.

I had to cut the cord.

* * *

The cupboards now stand bare. In the almost two months I have lived without him, I have not looked back – not for a moment. Even in that short time, I have forgotten what his presence felt like. I'm even beginning to wonder, sometimes, if he was real.

I fold the last of his shirts, gently and carefully and with a melancholy compassion for his hardships. As I place it on top of the rest, inside the third of the bags, I understand – completely – that he isn't coming back.

I tie a knot in the top of the bag. I wish his journey could have been easier. I know he'd been bad for me, but that he'd wished he hadn't been. I cry for him, knowing he'd done his best, but that he'd never felt it was enough. I let my tears flow, the way his never had.

198

When the bags are sealed and his scent is gone, I forgive him.
I forgive myself.
And I forgive the person I had once tried so desperately to be.

Acknowledgements

Though I have long known that I had some degree of aptitude, or even talent, for writing, I don't think I ever really imagined that I may one day become a published author. And yet, that day has arrived, and it is overwhelming. There are so many people without whom I would never have reached this point.

If you see your name below, know that although this is merely a token, your love and support have meant the world to me. If you don't, and you feel you should have, please accept that I was probably just running low on chocolate when I wrote this part, and that the omission was both unfortunate and accidental. Or, just maybe, it was personal.

Thank you Isobel, Emiliano, Tessa, Gabriella and Amilia, for your perseverance, your acceptance and your trust in me, even if I feel sometimes that I did not earn it. Now, with all said and done, you have my all, honestly and candidly. I wish I could have given it to you sooner, but I am grateful to have the opportunity now.

Ally, Marc, Kathy and Georgia, you are among the warmest, most wonderful people I have ever met. You encouraged me every step of the way, filling me with hope and inspiration when I needed it most. I love you all so very dearly.

Tanya, you are a loyal friend, loving and compassionate, not to mention amazingly talented. Thank you for always having a rainbow fart ready whenever it was needed.

My publishing team, without whom this book would never have been a reality: Angela, my editor; Ester and, prior to that, Elske, in the office; Jeremy; Jennifer, the publicity genius; and everyone else with whom I did not have the privilege of interacting personally, please know that I am nonetheless grateful.

Tania, you have been one of my closest friends for so long, despite all the factors that conspire to separate us. Thank you for not giving up on me, even when you had every reason to.

Karen and Shirley, for your warmth and generosity, always.

Marion, Tlaleng, Vikar, and the rest of the SRJC team, I met you after the manuscript had been completed, but your support has been a bastion. Keep fighting the good fight.

Michael and Karen, and family, for all the times you welcomed me into your home and your hearts.

Carol, thank you for your astute guidance and advice.

To my patients, each one of whom shared pieces of themselves with me and trusted me. In particular, Cheryl, Luella and Dean, Elain, Jenny, Simone, Ziggy and Justin. Your understanding and your support is overwhelming and I am so grateful.

May, you are just what medicine needs. Your idealism and your big, warm heart and your tremendous passion fill me with hope. Please don't ever let go of them. Remember – we can change the world. And we will.

Khin, I still struggle to find the words. 'Thank you' will have to do.

Natalie, you are ferocious and independent and simply just wonderful. And I am so glad to know that you have my back.

Rae, for your input and your sage advice I am ever grateful. You have done so much to help so many who are cutting their teeth in this craft, and I am thankful for all your concern and interest.

Sa'ar and Sharon, thank you for making me feel welcome when I had just about resigned myself to being forever an outcast. Your understanding, consideration and love have made such a difference not just in my life, but in so many.

Karyn, I do not even know where to begin. Without you, this entire book may still have just been a handful of lonely documents floating somewhere in the cloud. You gave me the push I needed, always believing in me, with genuine compassion and care. I am so very, very appreciative.

Elna, thank you for your warmth and your kindness and your

generosity of spirit. You are an amazing woman, and you look after so many.

To Rachel and to Casey, thank you both for commiserating, for listening, and for caring. And for being able to relate to all the guilt that comes from being 'Assigned Jewish at Birth' and/ or 'Jew-iiiiish'. I treasure your friendship.

Kelly, if I have not met you in person by the time this book is published, please remind me to chastise myself thoroughly. Actually, no. Forget that. I bet it's your fault, not mine. You are my spirit animal. Don't forget our pact, okay?

To my siblings, you beautiful motley crew. I adore the living crap out of you all. Eli, B, Alaine, Kate, Cammi, Bianca, The Roku, Elliot, Hugo, Tish, Trent, Germaine. You are stunning, gorgeous, phenomenal creatures.

Caitlin, you are doing such wonderful things, and you care so much. I am so fortunate to call you my friend.

To Ashley, the finest drill sergeant I have not yet had the privilege of meeting. I thank you, and so does Gotham City.

To Jessica, the finest veterinary tech that I have not yet had the privilege of meeting. You are exactly who I would want by my side when the zombies attack, as they inevitably will.

To my sisters: Charlotte, Vi, Lilith, Jess, Erin. You are the most exceptional, strongest, beautiful-est, and most magical women. I know I am never alone, and for that I thank you.

Allison, you gave me so much, and I will always be grateful. I want to tell you not to worry. Because, wherever we may find ourselves in life, I'm sure those words will fit for you. Wherever it ultimately is, though, I hope there will be happiness.

And, I'd like to clear the air, just to prove beyond owl doubt that I'm talonted at landing fowl puns – and I may claw anyone hoo suggests otherwise. And just so you know, I don't plan these things – I just wing it.

And lastly, but perhaps most importantly, two I must not neglect to thank, without which none of this would have been even remotely possible. My efforts would all have been for nought, and countless lives lost, even – likely mine among them. Coffee and chocolate, my heart is yours forever.

Glossary

asexual: someone who does not experience sexual attraction to others

assigned sex at birth: the classification of infants at birth as either male or female, usually based on inspection of the external genitalia. Thus, 'assigned male at birth' (AMAB) and 'assigned female at birth' (AFAB) should be used in place of such offensive and derogatory terms such as 'biological male/female', 'male/female bodied', 'natal male/female' or 'born male/female' when referring to trans people

binary: refers to the understanding of gender and sex as being exclusively either male or female

bisexual: an umbrella term describing people attracted to two genders, usually their own gender and another gender

cisgender: someone whose gender identity is wholly in line with their assigned sex at birth, i.e. who is not transgender. Referred to as 'cis' for short

cross-dresser: someone who, for whichever reason, dresses in clothing associated with the opposite gender. This is a form of gender expression – someone who is transgender is not cross-dressing

deadname: the name of a person who has since changed their name, especially a transgender person. May be used as a verb (deadnaming: referring to someone by their deadname instead of their chosen name)

demisexual: an identity on the asexual spectrum. It refers to someone who only experiences sexual attraction within the context of a strong emotional bond

dysphoria/gender dysphoria: anxiety, distress or discomfort (often profound) associated with or resulting from the incongruence between one's gender identity and assigned sex at birth

femme: an identity or expression that leans toward femininity

gender expression: the way in which one expresses one's gender, through clothing, hairstyles, behaviour, voice etc. Gender expression does not necessarily align with gender identity – for example, in the case of a cross-dresser

genderfluid: a gender identity that changes, i.e. is fluid

gender identity: one's internal sense of which gender one is. This is usually male, female, both, neither, or other. Everyone has a gender identity, including cisgender people

genderqueer: used to refer either to an identity or an expression that transgresses commonly accepted gender norms. It can be a blanket term

LGBT: lesbian, gay, bisexual, transgender; a blanket term for people who are not cisgender and heterosexual. Often expanded to LGBTQIA+ to include queer, questioning, intersex, and asexual people, as well as other identities

non-binary: an umbrella term for any gender identity that does not conform to the strict binary of being either male or female. Many non-binary people identify as transgender

pansexual: attracted to people of any gender, or attracted to people irrespective of their gender

queer: a general term for sexual and gender minorities that are not cisgender and heterosexual. Formerly used as a pejorative, but reclaimed by many people who identify as queer

sexual orientation: a person's enduring tendencies of attraction to others, for example straight, gay, lesbian, bisexual, pansexual. It is separate and distinct from gender identity

transgender: someone whose gender identity differs (completely or partially) from their assigned sex at birth

transvestite: formerly used to refer to cross-dressers, but nowadays often considered to be a pejorative term. Transgender people are not transvestites